HOW TO BE A

GOOFY JUGGLER

A COMPLETE COURSE IN JUGGLING MADE RIDICULOUSLY EASY!

By Bruce Fife

Piccadilly Books, Ltd.
COLORADO SPRINGS, COLORADO

ACKNOWLEDGMENTS
The Publisher is grateful to the following individuals and organizations for their generous assistance, and for their cooperation in making available pictorial materials: Bill Giduz, Ed Harris, Mark Ownby, Art Werger, Roger Dollarhide, Dick Franco, Marko Dzamtorski, Reg Bacon, Edward Jackman, Eric Berg, and The Variety Arts Photo Network. A special thanks is given to Bill Giduz of *Juggler's World* magazine for his invaluable support and assistance.

Piccadilly Books, Ltd.
P.O. Box 25203
Colorado Springs, CO 80936-5203 USA
info@piccadillybooks.com
www.piccadillybooks.com

Library of Congress Cataloging-in-Publication Data
Fife, Bruce
  How to be a goofy juggler.
  1. Juggling. I. Title.
GV1559.F48 1987 793.8   87-36149
ISBN-10: 0-941599-04-3
ISBN-13: 978-0-941599-04-7

Printed in the USA

TABLE OF CONTENTS

1

FUZZTAIL, WHANGDOODLE, AND GOOFBALL

"Hand over your money!" he said as his companion circled behind me.

I froze. I don't believe this—I'm being mugged! What should I do? Then the thought hit me; I'm a juggler and everyone likes jugglers—even muggers. Maybe if I tell them who I am they'll let me go. "You don't want to rob me," I said proudly. "I'm a juggler!"

"Shutup and give us your money!" demanded the mugger, flaunting a large club inches from my nose.

"But I am a juggler," I insisted. "Just let me borrow your clubs for a second and I'll show you."

"You touch this club, buddy, and I'll bat your brains out!"

At this point my mind went berserk (a common phenomenon with many jugglers). Since I wasn't carrying anything to prove to him I could juggle, I did the next best thing—I screamed and ran.

Before I could escape they tackled me and a rough and tumble fight commenced. With all my strength I vicously fought the attackers, but after several furious minutes of fighting, and 58 smacks on the side of my head with their clubs, I gave up. Searching through my pockets they found 43 cents and a half-eaten Hershey bar.

"You mean to tell me," asked one, "that you fought like that for 43 cents?"

"Gee," I said, "Is that all you wanted? If I'd known that, I would have given it to you. I thought you were after the $500 in my shoe."

Sometimes I say the stupidest things.

So what does this story have to do with juggling you ask? Absolutely nothing. I just wanted to get your attention. It sounds a lot better than beginning with "Here is a juggling ball. Toss it up and down . . . ."

Let me introduce myself. My name is Bruce Fife, but my friends call me Dopey—I mean Dr. Dropo. I'm a clown, juggler, balloonologist, lunatic, and all-round crazy person. I wasn't always this way. It just sort of happened to me when I learned how to juggle.

Some people say I'm crazy, a big goof, and a buffoon. I'm not really—I just act that way. I guess that's why I enjoy being a juggler. Jugglers can get away with acting goofy without appearing odd or different; it's expected of us.

I wrote this book because I realized that there are lots of other closet lunatics in the world just waiting to be freed. Now, for the first time since the creation of the whoopee cushion, people can release their inner craziness in public and feel good about it. Because all jugglers are recognized as crazy persons, as a juggler you will be able to do the most ridiculous things without feeling stupid!

When I discovered juggling, I knew right off that it was for me. All my life I'd wanted to do something better than anyone else. I didn't care what it was, just so I could get the recognition of being an expert in something. I tried all kinds of sports including, football, track, basketball, swimming, and even wrestling. In high school I went out for football and

played wide receiver. Durring the awards banquet at the end of the, year the coach presented me with the Rubber Hand Award because I dropped more balls than I caught. I tried track, and got an agonizing case of shin splints that made me walk like a saddlesore Texan. I was too short for the basketball team. The swimming coach told me I was too heavy to be a swimmer, and that's why I kept sinking to the bottom of the pool. He told me to try wrestling.

Wrestling required throwing myself around on the ground while hugging some sweaty guy I'd never met before and who hadn't taken a bath in six months. The encounter often ended with my faced smashed into the wrestling mat or into my opponent's armpit—neither of which I enjoyed.

I wasn't very successful in traditional sports but maybe, I thought, I could try something out of the ordinary—like fire eating, high-wire walking, or juggling. Fire eating was out because I get heartburn just eating marshmallows. High-wire walking was out because I get dizzy standing on my tiptoes. That left juggling, but juggling looked so hard. I had no idea even how to begin, so I didn't attempt it.

Later, when I saw a juggling class offered in the local paper, I decided to give it a try. To my surprise I found that learning to juggle wasn't difficult. Even I, "Mr. Rubber Hand," was able to juggle after one lesson. I was elated.

Juggling satisfied my desire to be good at something that few others could do. Most people can't juggle, not because it's hard to learn but because they've never tried. I found an activity that I could do better than 99.9 percent of the world's population. It made me special, but most of all it let me act crazy without looking stupid. I loved it.

Knowing how to juggle brought me immediate fame. Whenever people discovered my new talent, they pleaded for a demonstration. Not to disappoint them, I did what little juggling I could at the time. At first they looked at me in quiet amusement, but after 15 minutes of watching the same juggling pattern, they leaped with joy to see me stop. I was a success.

I could tell that even though juggling was interesting, I needed something else—some pizzazz, some humor. My skills were in their infancy at the time, so when people asked me to juggle, I spiced it up by throwing in a few jokes—and they loved it! I was a hit! It felt wonderful! These people were laughing at me. I'd been laughed at before, but this time I was *trying* to be funny.

At home, at work, at parties, visiting friends, everywhere I went if I let it leak out that I could juggle I was pushed into the spotlight. At the office one day, I was asked to do my stuff, so I pulled out an apple, borrowed an orange and a paperweight, and went at it, goofy faces and all, just as my supervisor walked by. Can you imagine how ridiculous I felt?

He casually looked, turned away to walk on, then jerked his head around in unbelief. "Fife, what are you doing?" he demanded.

"Er . . . ah . . ." How could I explain this?

"Were you juggling?"

I'm going to get it now, I thought. Fired for juggling on the job. Hesitantly I said, "Ah . . . yes, I was."

Cracking a smile he said, "Do some more."

I did, and a smiling cheering crowd soon gathered in my office—oh, the life of a juggler. Ever since then my supervisor has stopped looking at me as if I were genetically strange, he now understands and accepts the way I act because he knows I'm a juggler.

I began adding more jokes to my brief demonstrations. This was easy for a kooky guy like me. In fact, I find it hard not to goof around and create jokes while I'm juggling. That's one of the reasons I love it so much.

Before I knew it, I had enough material for a full 20 minute show. What was the logical conclusion? Yes, you guessed it—show biz. With the encouragement of family and friends, I began to give comedy juggling shows. My humor tends to be rather slapstick and silly, so I fit right into the clown image and thus "Dr. Dropo the Comic Juggler" was born.

How about you? Do you need an excuse to act crazy? Would you like the attention and praise that comes with being a goofy juggler? Would you like to be a funny juggling clown?

If you would, keep reading. Right now you're holding in your hands the key to learning how to juggle and how to make your juggling hilariously funny.

It doesn't matter if you're not the athletic type or if you're all thumbs. If I could learn to juggle, so can you. Remember, I received the Rubber Hand Award in high school because I couldn't hold on to the football. Anybody can juggle. It's not as hard as it's made out to be. All it takes is the proper instruction and a little practice. If you learned to ride a bicycle or even to walk, then you can learn to juggle.

But I must warn you, juggling has adverse side effects. The movement of the arms while juggling apparently pumps large quantities of blood into the elbows, stimulating the funny bone, which in turn affects the brain. This causes many jugglers to act strange and smile a lot (if you were strange before you started juggling—watch out!). Soon you will start to wear clownish looking clothes and tell jokes. Before you know it, people will stop laughing at your appearance and start laughing at your jokes. Whether you have a natural sense of humor or not, when you attempt to juggle everyone will laugh at you.

As funny as this may sound it does have some truth. There is a direct correlation between learning to juggle and acting funny. I don't know whether it's stimulation of the funny bone or not, but I have observed that those who take up juggling either become comedians or go crazy. In either case, they have a wonderful time.

Incidentally, you may have wondered why this chapter is titled "Fuzztail, Whangdoodle, and Goofball." These are nonsense words—a fitting description of this whole chapter. Besides, I didn't know what else to call it. In the next chapter I'll get serious (sort of) and guide you step-by-step through a system that's guaranteed to teach you how to juggle. This method is so easy that I've titled the next chapter "Juggling Made Easy."

2

JUGGLING MADE EASY

ANYBODY CAN JUGGLE

Have you ever admired the graceful, sure-handed moves of a juggler or the comical manipulations of a juggling clown and wondered how they can perform such seemingly difficult tricks? What's their secret—three hands? . . . No. What they do, so can you.

Anybody, and I mean *anybody*, can learn to juggle if they go about it in the right way! I don't care if the neighborhood kids call you Thumy because you're a klutz or even if you really do have all thumbs, you can learn how to juggle. Juggling is like magic, once you know the "secret" it's simple. What is this closely guarded secret? The secret can be summed up in one word—persistence! That's right, persistence, there is no hidden movement or trick that will make juggling easy. You will have to practice. "But wait!" you say. "This chapter is titled Juggling Made Easy, what's the big idea?"

The fact is, the speed at which you will learn to juggle will be determined by the amount of practice you put into it. But don't worry, in this chapter I will give you a step-by-step method that will make learning to juggle enormously easier than trying on your own.

How long does it take to learn? Everybody is different, and the time you will need will depend on your natural ability and your determination.

I've found that those who pick up juggling the quickest happen to be between four and seven feet tall, weigh under 440 pounds, have two hands (one right and one left), can see at least one foot beyond the end of their nose, can chew gum and whistle at the same time, walk on their hands with their toes crossed, wiggle their ears, and sing "Let Me Call You Sweetheart, Because I Can't Remember Your Name" while bouncing on a pogo stick and playing the violin. I can teach this type of person to juggle in less than five minutes. If you don't happen to be one of these people, it will take a little longer.

If, however, you possess *any* of these characteristics (like a right and a left hand) you have the natural ability to become a wonderful juggler. Don't let this inborn talent go to waste!

The system I use to teach juggling has proven successful for hundreds of satisfied students. Students of all ages, physical characteristics, and varying amounts of uncoordination have been taught to juggle using my system.

The method I use may actually be too easy for you! In fact, it may be so easy that it feels like cheating. If you're worried about learning too fast and would like to take more time, you can skip the rest of this chapter and try practicing on your own, using the trial-and-error-method. For the rest of you, who don't mind cheating—keep reading.

I use a progressive system to teach juggling. Trying to learn to juggle three balls all at once is overwhelming and discouraging. You only have two hands (at least most of you) and keeping three (or more) balls moving continuously in the air cannot be learned just by picking up some balls and tossing them around a few times. If the number of balls is decreased, tossing and catching become much easier. (I figured this one out all by myself.) The mind is also free to concentrate on the proper way to throw and catch the balls without being overwhelmed.

I will guide you through a series of steps beginning with only one ball. You will learn the correct (and easiest) way to throw and catch it. Once you have mastered one-ball juggling, you will move up to two balls. The next step is two and a half balls, and so on until you have developed enough control to tackle three-ball juggling.

TOOLS OF THE TRADE

Picture yourself surrounded by amused onlookers as you effortlessly toss around balls, apples, and eggs. Listen to their delighted laughter as you gleefully throw razor sharp knives and axes past your skull. Oh, the thrill of it all!

Before you can learn how to juggle, you need to have something to juggle. You don't need to buy any special equipment. Every household comes fully equipped with its own juggling apparatus (or props, as they say in the business). What do you use? Just about anything you can hold in your hand: tennis balls, golf balls, baseballs, meatballs, bowling pins, potatoes, melons, rolled-up socks, underwear, spitwads, parakeets, gerbils, Jello, doohickies, gizmos, and thingumabobs—almost anything.

If you're the challenging sort, you may try axes, machetes, flaming torches, chain saws, and bowling balls. But please be careful, especially with bowling balls—they can leave dents in the floor, your foot, and the cat. Knives and chain saws, on the other hand, don't leave unsightly dents and are favored by many three-fingered, one-eyed jugglers. Razor-sharp balls have traditionally been favored, however, they are much more dangerous than knives because you never know where the edge is.

I recommend tennis balls, baseballs, lacrosse balls, or hand-sized bean bags. Small spherical objects like these are the easiest to use. Objects that are not basically spherical, such as juggling clubs (cousins of the bowling pin) and rings, require a spinning motion to be kept in balance. Before attempting to juggle nonspherical objects you should first learn to juggle with balls or bean bags.

The best type of ball is one that is small enough so that two of them can fit comfortably in the palm of your hand (about two to three inches in diameter). Basketballs take a bit more skill to handle.

A heavy ball is more manageable than a light one. Lightweight balls, such as ping pong balls and racketballs, tend to bounce in the palm of the hand when they are being caught, increasing the difficulty of juggling.

In my juggling classes I tell my students that if they think they will have any trouble learning to juggle, to practice with heavy balls. Generally the heavier the balls are, the easier they are to control. One of my students took my advice to heart and showed up at the next class carrying three bowling balls!

I then began to tell my students not to use something too heavy, either. Another student showed up with three beans— not bean bags, just three beans. Although it may be possible to learn to juggle using things like this, don't be ridiculous. Save the kooky stuff until after you start stimulating your funny bones.

The best balls to use are both small and slightly heavy. Some balls are made specifically for juggling and work very well. Lacrosse balls are popular with jugglers. These types of balls can be purchased from novelty shops or juggling suppliers. If nothing else is available, tennis balls or rolled-up socks will do.

For a beginner, I would recommend bean bags. They are relatively heavy and don't bounce around in the hand, making them very easy to catch and control. Another important feature of the bean bag that beginners will appreciate is that when dropped they won't bounce or roll away.

Balls have a natural attraction for low, dark places, such as under the couch or down the basement stairs. You'll be amazed at the ingenious spots balls find to hide in. I have dozens of balls hiding around my home. If you start out using balls, be prepared to spend half of your time looking for the ones that run away.

Bean bags can be homemade or you can find them at your neighborhood juggling supplier. If you learn to juggle using bean bags, you will also be able to juggle balls.

Throughout the rest of this chapter I will explain the steps of juggling using the term "ball" but you can use anything you like.

Kornballs

You don't need to go out and buy a set of expensive juggling balls or bean bags to get started. A couple of handfuls of unpopped popcorn and three gym socks (preferably unscented) will make a nice cheap set of kornballs.

Although not pretty, kornballs are just the right size and weight for juggling. They also mold to the shape of the hand on contact, which keeps them from rolling or bouncing off your palms. Which is nice if you're trying to juggle.

Bean bags and their cousins, the kornballs, are preferred by most beginners over the usual tennis balls. Kornballs fit jugglers. Korny jokes complement kornballs (aren't all jugglers korny?).

To make your own personalized set of kornballs, start by gathering the materials—three socks, three rubber bands, one package of cheap popcorn (or split peas or dried beans). Small socks work best. If you have big feet or are a circus clown, borrow three socks from someone else. When they ask you "Why *three* socks?" say: 1) it's a family secret, 2) two are for you and one is for a friend, or 3) you're going to juggle them. They will probably believe either the first or second answer, the third is too bizarre.

Now fill the toe of one sock with popcorn. Don't get carried away, you don't want to toss around cannon balls. Fill it just enough to make a racketball-sized ball, about half of a cup worth (Figure 2-1).

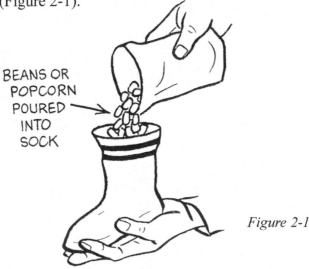

BEANS OR
POPCORN
POURED
INTO
SOCK

Figure 2-1

Tie a rubber band around the bulb of the sock as shown in Figure 2-2.

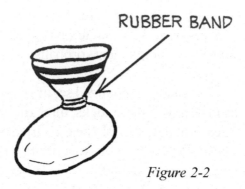

RUBBER BAND

Figure 2-2

Pull the top of the sock down over the balled end (Figure 2-3).

Figure 2-3

Twist the neck of the sock and fold it over the ball again (Figure 2-4).

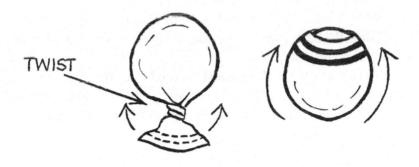

Figure 2-4

If you have big feet and are using your own socks, you may end up with excess sock. Repeat the twisting and folding until the sock loses its "tail."

You now have one kornball ready to go. Feel the comfortable fit, the soft exterior. Give it a toss, watch it soar. It's like witnessing the flight of an eagle . . . egg.

Don't get too involved with it yet. Make the other two kornballs, then continue.

Figure 2-5

JUGGLING THE EASY WAY

If you would like to learn the easiest and quickest way to juggle, this is it. Take one ball in your right hand, another in your left hand, and put a third ball in your mouth. While holding the balls in this position, swing your arms rapidly and jump up and down.

This is by far the easiest method I know of to juggle. Unfortunately, it's not too impressive. If you want to learn to juggle in the traditional manner by tossing and catching the balls, keep reading.

THE DROP

To start off your juggling instruction, let's practice the first and most popular trick known to jugglers. Take one ball in your right hand, holding it loosely between your fingers. Now turn the palm down and let the ball drop to the floor. This trick is commonly referred to as "the drop."

The drop is performed with one or more balls and in many different ways. The easiest is the simple drop just described. Other methods involve much more fanfare and acrobatics, such as throwing the ball into the air and trying to catch it before it hits the floor. For more excitement you may add running into the couch, hitting your shins on the coffee table, or slipping on the rug and falling on your face. You may also try bouncing it off the top of your head or have it bounce off the wall and rebound off your nose, or simply bobbling it between your hands before dropping it. These techniques take a great deal of practice, and a skilled juggler can drop as many as three or four balls at one time.

Dropping tricks are very common, and you must master them all in order to be a respectable juggler. Practice the simple drop a couple of times to get the feel of it. Surprisingly, most people pick up this trick real fast.

All jugglers, no matter how proficient they are, drop props; it's part of the game. There's no way around it. Now that you have mastered the drop, let's go on to more serious juggling.

THE CASCADE

Do you remember the first time you drove a car? Can you recall the joy you felt during your first unassisted bicycle ride? Do you remember the day you took your first step; nervous, unsure of yourself, reluctant to let go of your mom's hand? Your legs trembled with excitement as you released your grip and took you first step or two. A thrilling experience! Ah yes—who could forget such moments?

Learning how to juggle is just as thrilling, and is really no more difficult than learning how to walk. Like walking, once you've learned how to juggle, the skill remains with you forever. However, no matter how carefully I explain each step or how much detail I give, you will probably find some way to goof it up. So, to avoid as much fumbling as possible, please read the following explanation carefully and keep repeating to yourself, "Any bozo can do it."

Your goal for the rest of this chapter is to learn how to juggle using the cascade pattern. The cascade is the basic three-ball juggling pattern that all jugglers use. It's considered a rest position between the more difficult tricks. Once you have mastered the essentials of the cascade, you can branch off and learn more difficult patterns, tricks, and best of all—goofy jokes and stunts.

Begin by putting two balls in your left hand and one ball in your right. Now lift the left hand high above your head and arch your back as far as possible. Take a second to check to make sure you're positioned correctly, see Figure 2-6.

Figure 2-6

In this position, open the left hand and let the two balls fall to the floor. This will leave you with only one ball in your right hand; this is where we will start. You will begin step one, using a single ball, and gradually progress to step six where you will practice the cascade using three balls.

Step One

Before doing anything else, imagine two spots at about forehead level, one just to the right of your head and the other just to the left, see Figure 2-7. Both spots should be about a foot in front of your face. *These are your control points and are very important!*

Figure 2-7

Figure 2-8

Take one ball in your right hand and hold it with the elbow bent at about stomach level (Figure 2-8). Figure 2-9 illustrates this position as you would see it from your perspective.

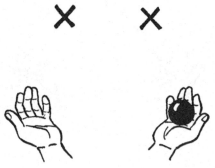

Figure 2-9

Toss the ball up and across to the imaginary spot on the left side of your forehead (Figure 2-10). When it comes down, catch it in your left hand.

Toss the ball from your left hand up to the imaginary spot at the right side of your forehead. As it falls, catch it with your right hand (Figure 2-11). The ball has now made one round trip in a lazy figure 8 pattern (∞) see Figure 2-12.

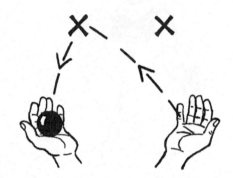

Figure 2-10

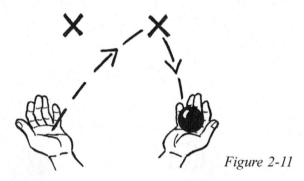

Figure 2-11

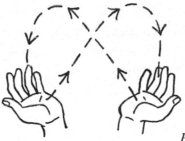

Figure 2-12

Practice this pattern, making sure that the ball hits the imaginary spots at each side of your face. Don't throw the ball too high or too low. Make your throws as consistent as possible by focusing your attention on these spots; don't look at your hands. Right now it's not much of a problem if you don't get the ball to hit the spots exactly, but it will become vital as you work up to three balls, so practice it right.

"Juggling is catching" is a common saying among jugglers. Although this is a clever play on words, it would be more accurate to say "Juggling is throwing up." That, however, doesn't quite have the same appeal as the first saying.

By far the most important thing to learn when starting to juggle is how to throw the balls properly. A misthrown ball can be all but impossible to catch, no matter how skilled you are.

Balls that are thrown correctly just seem to fall into the proper hand. Catching is more of a natural response and comes easily. If you fail to catch a ball, the most likely reason is that you threw it incorrectly. That's why I emphasize throwing the balls to the imaginary spots. If you do this, the balls will travel in a path that allows them to end up in the proper place and to be kept moving at a steady rhythm. As you practice, concentrate 90 percent of your effort on throwing. If you do this, you will soon be juggling three balls with confidence.

Also, as you practice, make sure not to reach up to grab the ball as it comes down. Let the ball fall into your hand. Make it a point never to raise your hands above chest level when either throwing or catching the balls. This is done for two reasons: 1) it helps regulate your timing, and 2) it keeps the BO from escaping from under your armpits.

Continue to practice this step until you feel comfortable with it.

Step Two

Now that you have mastered one-ball juggling, you can try two balls. Put one ball into each hand. Keep your elbows bent and your hands at stomach level.

Throw the ball in the right hand up to the imaginary spot at the left side of your head (Figure 2-13). When the ball reaches this spot, toss the ball that is in the left hand toward the imaginary spot at the right side of your head (Figure 2-14). After tossing the ball out of the left hand, quickly catch with the left hand the ball thrown by the right hand (Figure 2-15). Finally, the right hand will catch the ball thrown by the left.

You have just made a simple exchange. The ball that started in the right hand is now in the left and vice versa.

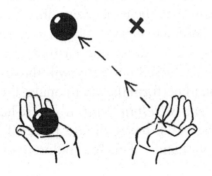

Figure 2-13

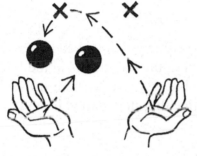

Figure 2-14

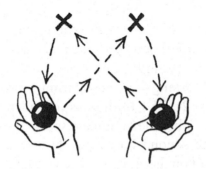

Figure 2-15

Repeat this sequence, starting with the right hand and continue until you can catch the balls every time.

It is important to throw each ball as close to the imaginary spots as possible. I cannot emphasize this point too much. A ball that is not tossed correctly will throw off your timing, causing you to perform the ever popular drop.

Dr. Dropo's Helpful Hint: If you're having a hard time catching the balls, try sewing a piece of Velcro onto the palms of your hands. This is a foolproof method that works every time.

Step Three

Repeat the procedure you followed in step two, but this time start by throwing the ball that is in the left hand first. This sounds easy, but it's a little more difficult than you might think. Practice this step until you can catch the balls every time.

Step Four

Take one ball in each hand. This time imagine an invisible third ball in your right hand, so that you have one real ball in your left hand and one real ball and one invisible ball in your right (Figure 2-16).

Begin by tossing the real ball from your right hand in the pattern (Figure 2-17). Continue as you did in step two. When the first ball reaches the imaginary spot at the left side of your head, toss the second ball from the left hand toward the imaginary spot on the right. Quickly catch the first ball with the left hand (Figure 2-18).

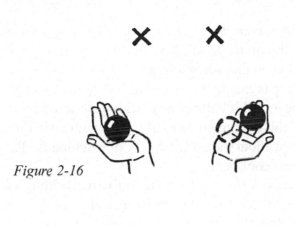

Figure 2-16

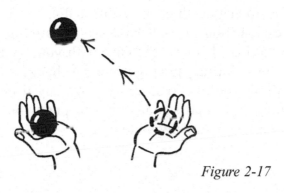

Figure 2-17

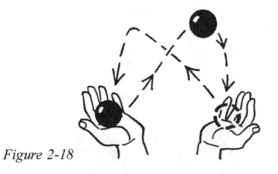

Figure 2-18

As the second ball reaches the imaginary spot on the right, toss the invisible third ball from your right hand and catch the descending second ball.

This step is exactly like step two except that you pretend to throw the invisible ball before catching the second ball. The purpose of this movement is to give you practice in throwing a third ball without the added worry of catching it. Practice until you feel confident.

Dr. Dropo's Helpful Hint: If you're really imaginative, you can use three invisible balls and skip on to step six where I explain the three-ball exchange. Most people find it easy to juggle three invisible balls, but it isn't very impressive. Some people have such a hard time they can't even do this. If that's the case with you, try using three machetes. You may not juggle very well, but your audience will think you're a real cutup, and they'll probably die laughing. OK, that's enough of this punny business, start practicing with one invisible ball.

Step Five

In this step you do the same thing as you did in step four except that you replace the invisible ball with a real one (Figure 2-19).

Figure 2-19

Proceed as you did in the last step. When you get to the point of throwing the third ball, concentrate on the accuracy of the throw. Make sure it goes to the imaginary spot at the left side of your head. Don't worry about catching it right now, let it drop to the floor.

The purpose of this step is to give you practice actually throwing the third ball and making the throw correct. Check yourself as you practice, making sure each of the three balls hit the imaginary spots.

For some of you this step will come easily and you will naturally move on to the next and final step.

Step Six

If you have practiced steps one through five and can perform them with confidence, this step will come with relative ease.

Pick up all three balls. Hold one ball in your left hand and two balls in the right (Figure 2-19). Do the same thing that you did in step five, but this time catch the third ball as it comes down. Make sure you throw the ball that is already in your hand before catching the next ball. Continue by tossing and catching each ball in succession. DON'T STOP! Keep tossing the balls in the ∞ pattern (Figure 2-20).

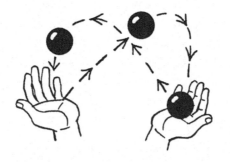

Figure 2-20

You will notice that after the first two throws the right hand is doing the same thing as the left—catching and throwing the balls, that's all there is to it. If you can do this without stopping, then you're juggling!

Did you feel the excitement and the thrill of your first juggle? Did you notice the uncontrollable urge to act goofy? Did you look goofy? If so, you're on your way to becoming a talented goofy juggler. Move over Jay Leno— a new comic has been born!

If, however, you managed to look like a bozo and couldn't juggle three balls, don't feel bad try again. The step from two to three balls is a big one and generally requires more practice than the other steps. Expect to spend some time working on this last step. If you feel that you're having more difficulty than you should, back up a step or two and practice that step again.

Most problems are caused by not throwing the balls to the imaginary points each time. As I said before, the throw is very important. Concentrate on throwing the balls to these spots and don't worry so much about catching. That will come as your throws improve.

As you begin practicing with three balls, don't expect to throw them and automatically begin juggling continuously. At first you may complete only four or five throws before the inevitable drop occurs. Pick them up and try again. With practice you'll gradually lengthen the time you can juggle before dropping. I find it helpful to set periodic goals for my students. Beginning with say five continuous throws and catches and then six, seven, ten, fifteen and so on. By practicing this way, before you know it, you will be juggling like a pro—or at least like a goofy clown.

Dr. Dropo's Helpful Hint: If you're having problems throwing and catching three balls, it could mean that you're leaning off balance. To correct your balance, stick out your tongue and try again. Many beginning jugglers find this technique very helpful. Hey, don't laugh, if juggling can stimulate the funny bone then the tongue can be used for balance. I think I've been juggling too long . . . .

3

SIMPLE TRICKS AND STUNTS

HOW TO JUGGLE
WITHOUT REALLY TRYING

You've read the last chapter, followed my instructions, and now can juggle three balls in the cascade pattern—right? So what do you do now? Start demonstrating your amazing abilities for thrilled audiences? Not quite. Watching someone toss and catch three gym socks is interesting, but you wouldn't want to make an evening of it. To spice up the basic cascade and make your juggling interesting, you will need to add tricks and humor. It's learning variations on the cascade that makes juggling exciting and enjoyable.

But wait, you say. You're still having trouble with the cascade. Don't worry, before I go any further, let me describe a different juggling pattern that any goof can master. This pattern is called the *underarm exchange* and is much easier to learn than the cascade, yet is not seen very often because it is not as versatile. But if you can handle this technique, then you can call yourself an underarm juggler.

The Underarm Exchange

The underarm exchange is a juggling pattern completely different from the cascade and much easier. You should be able to master it in just a few minutes, whether you were able to do the cascade or not.

When doing the three-ball cascade, you only use two hands to manipulate three balls. A difficult task for many novices. With the underarm exchange you cheat and use not only your hands but both of your your armpits as well, making the whole affair rather simple.

Begin by placing one ball under your left armpit. Let both of your arms hang loosely at your sides. This will keep enough pressure on the ball to hold it in place. Hold one

ball in your right hand and one in your left. Now begin juggling by taking the ball in the left hand and placing it under the right armpit. As your left hand drops back to your side, release the ball in the left armpit and let it drop into the left hand. The right hand now does the same thing. Put the ball that is in your right hand into your left armpit and catch the next ball in your right hand as it drops to your side. Continue this exchange as long as you wish, or until you fall asleep, whichever comes first.

This juggling movement looks easy, and it is, but you can make it look harder by adding some body movement. Lift one leg or try shuffling from one leg to the other, or bend your knees and raise and lower your body as you juggle.

After you're able to do the underarm exchange, then what? Go back and practice the cascade. The cascade is to an experienced juggler what walking is to a runner. The cascade is used as a mobile rest position between the more difficult tricks and juggling humor. Tricks and pattern variations can be performed one after another, but typically they are separated by the cascade. This is particularly true with comedy juggling where a specific joke accompanies each particular juggling movement. In this chapter and others I will describe several tricks that you can combine with the cascade to give you variety, provide new challenges, and increase the potential for juggling humor.

JUGGLING JOLLIES

I will now describe some jolly juggling tricks, or what I call dumb tricks. Why do I call them dumb? Because it would be stupid to call them smart, that's why. These are silly tricks that can be performed by anyone who knows how to do the cascade. Some may be so off-the-wall you won't want to try them. But if you can cascade three balls, you will, with a little practice, be able to do all the tricks in this chapter.

Face Juggling

Face juggling is one of the easiest tricks to do once you've learned the three-ball cascade. Face juggling is simply contorting the face rhythmically as you toss and catch the balls. You are, in a sense, juggling your face. Many people do it unconsciously anyway while they juggle.

Look at yourself in the mirror. Make a few goofy faces, if one isn't already present. Don't hold back. Flex and stretch those muscles. Now begin juggling. Flex and relax the muscles, pull them to one side and then to the other. That's it. Let me add a word of warning, make sure no one is watching—it could be embarrassing. When you show others this trick, it still could be embarrassing but by then you'll be too kooky to care. But for now, practice alone.

Got it? Now rush out and demonstrate to your friends. After witnessing this trick, they'll agree that juggling has affected your brain and they'll call you a goofy juggler. Take a bow. Easy wasn't it?

You'll rely on the funny face technique many times to help make other tricks and jokes funnier. If you don't get a laugh after telling a joke, make a goofy face. Nine times out of ten, adding this little bit of physical buffoonery will enhance your joke and gain you a greater response.

Sometimes the response will be more laughter; at other times it will be rotten tomatoes. But at least you'll get a reaction, anything is better than stony-faced stares.

Tongue Juggling

Without using your hands, extend your tongue out of your mouth and wag it back and forth in rhythm with your juggling. This can be a very funny sight, but please avoid drooling. Nobody likes a slobbering juggler.

This trick can be performed solo, or you can invite several friends over and do it all together. Group tongue juggling—the ultimate in friendly get-togethers. Add chips and a few dips and turn it into a goof party or wacky wingding.

On One Leg

Stand with your feet together, back straight, and begin juggling. Now slowly lift one foot off the floor—you've got it. Keep juggling. Lift the foot up higher . . . higher . . . higher. That's it! Make a goofy face.

Richard Simmons Juggle

While juggling, alternately lift each leg straight out to the side and count "One and two and three and . . ." Try imitating a squeaky Simmons voice. Wearing leotards and curling your hair also help.

Germ Juggling

Are you still having troubles with the cascade but want to do some fancy tricks for your friends? This is the trick for you. Instead of juggling balls or bean bags, you can juggle germs. Yes, germs.

Germ juggling is very simple. All you do is take three or more germs and juggle them.

Begin by sneezing into your hands. The sneeze will provide abundant microscopic germs to work with. Now start tossing the germs back and forth. Since germs are so tiny, it will be impossible for anyone to see them, but never mind that, just move those arms and juggle.

This is a nifty trick because it can be done almost anywhere, while waiting in line, driving the car, at work, or when you're walking down the street. However, you will undoubtedly attract what scientists refer to as "gawkers"— curious people who will stop and gawk at you. If anyone asks what you're doing, tell them you're juggling. This answer will satisfy most people, but a few knuckleheads may ask "What are you juggling?" Simply reply "germs" and they'll leave you alone.

Advanced Germnastics

Once you've mastered the simple germ juggle, you can combine it with other tricks and perform germnastics. Any trick that is possible with balls, and many that are impossible, can be performed using germs. Try these simple maneuvers: standing on one foot, under-the-leg toss, behind-the-back toss, a double somersault with a back flip, swan dive off the couch landing in the splits followed

Goofy juggler Rich Hayes. Hayes was considered by some to be one of the most intelligent jugglers ever. Notice the large development of his brain. Recent scientific research suggests that the brain is actually a large muscle and can be enlarged through proper exercise. It is theorized that vigorous movement of the tongue, which is attached to the brain muscle, combined with goofy actions, such as juggling or running for political office, can result in a swelled head.

by rolling over into a headstand—remember, don't stop juggling your germs. Some of your friends may think you're having a mental breakdown, but just explain to them that you're a juggler. They'll understand.

One Ball High

This trick is probably the easiest variation of the cascade pattern there is, and you should be able to master it with just a few of minutes of practice.

While tossing the balls in the cascade pattern, throw one of the balls several feet higher than normal. If you toss it with the right hand, it should go to the left side of the body. Catch each of the other two balls, one in each hand, and wait for the third ball to come down (a half second or so). As it falls, it should pass the imaginary spot on the left side of your head. Toss the ball in the left hand to the other imaginary spot on your right, catch the descending ball, and continue to juggle normally.

This explanation sounds a lot harder than it really is. Just try it, all you're really doing is the cascade with one ball tossed unusually high.

Hiccups

Continually toss one ball high, as described above. As you throw the high ball say, "HICK!"

Reverse Juggling

Turn around and juggle backwards and you'll be doing reverse juggling . . . I didn't say all of these tricks would be funny now, did I?

Flea Juggling

While juggling in the cascade, scratch yourself between throws. Make it part of the pattern: toss-toss-scratch, toss-toss-scratch.

This is a handy trick to learn in case an unexpected itch sneaks up on you in the middle of a demonstration. The audience will think it's part of the performance.

Invariably an uncontrollable itch will develop once you start juggling in front of a crowd, but if you've prepared yourself beforehand, you will be ready for it and will scratch with confidence.

The Toss-In

Here's an impressive stunt that will get your audience involved. Give one of your balls to an observer. With one ball in each of your hands, have the observer toss the third ball to you. As he or she does so, toss one of the balls you are holding into the cascade pattern and catch the incoming ball. Continue to toss and catch the balls in the cascade. This is a simple trick if the ball is thrown within reach.

Non-jugglers, however, are notoriously clumsy and generally can't hit the broad side of a bum. As a result, you may have to run around in an attempt to catch the stray ball. Poorly thrown balls, however, can add some humor. Let the incoming ball bounce off your forehead (this may happen anyway) or while racing to grab a wild ball, slip, trip, and flip onto your face. Everyone will laugh. You have proven to them that you are a goofy juggler.

The Teeth Grab

Some tricks involve unique catches or balancing techniques. The teeth grab is a catch that can be used with either balls or bean bags.

*Two left hand?!... No. Comic juggler Reg Bacon, alias Mr. Slim,
contorts to juggle three balls around his back.*

If you've ever tossed popcorn up in the air and caught it in your mouth, you know how this trick works. The only difference is that you use balls—not as tasty as popcorn, but the technique is the same.

While juggling, toss one ball high above your head. As it comes down, catch it between your teeth. Bite securely, tilt your head forward, and show the audience. For that extra laugh, bring the other two balls up and cover your eyes, creating a goony-looking face. Non-jugglers are always amused at this sight.

Bean bags work best because they are easier to bite onto, but you can use almost any prop you want.

Warning! Do not attempt this trick with bowling balls. Bowling balls will leave an impression on your audience and on your nose. (Hey, if you're crazy enough to read this book, you're crazy enough to try anything.)

The Nose Balance

This stunt is called the nose balance and NO—you do not balance your nose! You balance a bean bag on top of your nose.

Bend your head back and rest the bag on your schnozzola. This trick is called the one-bag balance. Once you've mastered balancing one bag, try balancing two by placing a second bag on top of the first. You can also try a three-bag balance.

If you have trouble doing this trick, your nose may be too big. Try flattening out your nose with a couple of raps from a hammer. If you still have trouble, instead of bean bags try using giant wads of bubble gum. They stick better.

Head Balance

This is very similar to the nose balance, but instead of balancing the bags on your nose you balance them on top of your head.

Try juggling three balls while keeping three bags stacked up on your head. You can call yourself "Spike."

Head Bounce

Instead of balancing a ball on your head, bounce it off your head while you're juggling. This is a cute looking trick that will please any audience. Practice using bean bags or balls at first.

Once you've become proficient with bouncing a ball off your head, try using other objects. This will add even more excitement to the act. Experiment hitting your head with a cabbage or a watermelon. The audience will love it. But you will need to practice a bit first. Bouncing these objects feels significantly different then bean bags or soft rubber balls.

Fruit Toss

If you can do the cascade, you can juggle many different types of objects. Fruits are popular with jugglers. Anything that is more or less round can be juggled like a ball. Try juggling apples, tomatoes, grapefruit, cantaloupes, and artichokes.

Eggs are fun. Try juggling three of these white jewels. You can perform all of the tricks described in this chapter, like the teeth catch, although you may wind up with egg on your face. Try hitting yourself on the head with the eggs— it's a mess of laughs.

Eating the Apple

The famous apple eating trick is without a doubt the most popular of all juggling tricks. Sooner or later you'll be asked to perform it, so let me explain how it's done.

Start with two balls and one apple. First check the apple for signs of worms. Once you've started to juggle, it will be too late. In all the excitement of juggling and eating, you won't notice the presence of the little alien until after you've dissected it with your teeth. Such an incident could lead to uncontrollable loss of appetite and the dumping your cookies onto the stage. An unpleasant sight for most audiences.

To perform the apple eating trick, start with the cascade. As you juggle, catch the apple and quickly take a bite out of it before tossing it back into the pattern. At first it may be helpful if you toss the balls higher than normal to allow you a little additional time to complete the move. As your speed improves, you'll be able to do this trick while juggling at your usual height.

Practicing this stunt can become messy, so you may want to try it using three bean bags and just go through the motion of taking a bite. You can call this "eating the bag," but be careful—bean bags taste terrible!

For variety try eating a block of cheese, or a turnip, a meatball, or a turkey leg.

Over-the-Top

This trick is a little more difficult to learn than the others mentioned so far, but it's a slick looking move that has a variety of uses.

In this trick you juggle two balls in the normal cascade pattern while tossing one ball over the top of the other two. Start with the cascade. While juggling, instead of tossing one ball in the normal crisscross pattern, lob it up in a high arc over the the pattern. Catch it with the opposite hand and continue juggling (Figure 3-1). Practice this several times using the same throwing hand, then try it with the other hand.

Figure 3-1

When you can do over-the-top with either hand, try combining the moves so the ball will be tossed back and forth continuously over the top of the others. I call this trick *ping-pong.*

As you do ping-pong, move your head from side to side in rhythm with the upper ball. Now contort your face and look dopey. (This is what kept me out of the army.)

The Claw

Here's a trick that will require a little practice. Clawing is an alternate method of catching and throwing the balls in the cascade pattern. It's harder than the regular cascade but looks slick.

For a single handed claw, start by juggling normally in the cascade pattern. The claw is done by grabbing a ball out of the air with the hand held palm down, as if you were clawing (Figure 3-2). As you juggle, you will "claw" one ball and return it to the pattern without missing a beat.

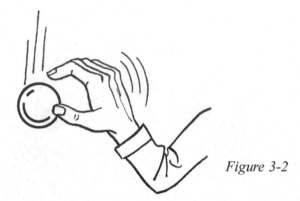

Figure 3-2

As soon as you grab the ball, quickly swing your hand up and let the ball go, moving your hand away so the ball can return to the pattern. Keep juggling and try it again.

Grabbing and tossing the ball in a clawed hand will feel terribly awkward at first. But do it anyway.

Practice clawing by using one hand for now. It's not really a hard movement but will take some time getting used to. Once you've learned clawing with one hand, try it with the other.

Combine both hands and claw right-left. Work up to a continuous three-ball claw. You'll have to move rapidly to keep the balls off the floor, but it looks flashy.

Clawing can be used to add variety to your juggling and can be combined with clever humor. A typical comic bit using the claw is the IRS gag, which goes as follows:

Begin by juggling in the cascade and tell your listeners, "In the old days, the IRS took only a little of our money." Do a single claw and say "Gimme!"

Continue juggling in the cascade and say, "But now they want everything." Go into continuous clawing as you say, "Gimme, gimme, gimme!"

The Shower

No book on juggling would be complete without describing the shower. The shower is a juggling pattern in which the balls are tossed in a large circle. Non-jugglers are most familiar with this pattern because it's the one always depicted in cartoons. The shower, however, is not an easy pattern to learn, but I'll explain what I feel is the easiest way to learn it.

Begin with two balls in your right hand. Toss one ball after the other in a circular pattern moving counterclockwise (Figure 3-3). Don't do anything with your left hand yet. Use only the right hand to toss and catch the balls. Practice this step until you can work two balls continuously with one hand.

Once you feel confident tossing and catching two balls with one hand, add your left hand. Raise the left hand

Figure 3-3

slightly above the right. The right hand will toss each ball in a high arc. The left hand will catch it and lightly toss it over to the right hand (Figure 3-4). After practicing two balls in one hand, this move will be easy.

Now you're ready to practice the the three-ball shower. Start with two balls in your right hand and one ball in your left. Beginning with the right hand toss them, one at a time, in the circular pattern and keep going. That's all there is to it. It looks and sounds easy but will take a while to master.

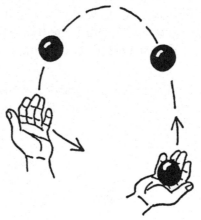

Figure 3-4

The Dance Juggle

To do the dance juggle, move the entire body in a dance-like motion while juggling. Combine the waltz, rumba, tap dancing, or clogging with juggling. Or do a more expressive modern dance. How about break dancing? Juggle while jumping up, and come down into a belly flop on the floor, twist and spin on your elbow, knee, and head—remember to keep juggling the whole time. I guarantee that on a busy street you'll stand out in the crowd.

If you find break juggling too difficult, you can do a modified version. Juggle three bottles, breaking each one in turn over your skull—a very funny trick, however, it has a tendency to produce large, unsightly nodules on the head and may cause you to stagger around with your tongue hanging out and your eyes crossed. But anything is worth doing for a laugh—right? How do you think most jugglers get so dizzy anyway?

What's this? Three typical jugglers on their way to the beach? No —this is the unique juggling trio Airjazz (left to right) Kezia Tenenbaum, Jon Held, Peter Davison.

"Here come the girls! Try to act natural." Greg Cortopassi and Bruce Guettich juggle on the slops.

Eric Berg, juggling surfer

Joggling

Combine jogging and juggling in a unique form of exercise known as joggling. An easy way to start out is to try juggling while running in place. If you can handle that, step out and start jogging. It's really easier than it looks. If you can do break juggling, this will be a snap.

Joggling is very popular with many jugglers, and has developed into a sport by itself. Joggling races are run all across the country. The distances most typically run are 100 meters and the mile, but jogglers have also competed in marathons. Joggler Albert Lucas is one such marathoner who has completed the 26 mile Boston Marathon without a single drop! I wish I could say the same thing about my cousin Soapy.

Every year the International Jugglers Association (IJA) sponsors a joggling competition in which jugglers from all over the world gather to compete for the unofficial title of "world's fastest joggler." Some jugglers have gone so far as to joggle on ice skates. Others joggle on roller skates, skis, and even surfboards. I prefer to use the lawn chair myself.

If you really want to be a goofy juggler, put on a cowboy hat, a pair of dress shoes, jogging shorts, and a necktie and go out on the street joggling. If you do that, you're more than goofy—you're crazy!

4

SMOOTIES

EMBARRASSING MOMENTS

You've mastered a few tricks, memorized some jokes and are invited, or even paid, to demonstrate your goofy skills in front of an audience. What would be the most embarrassing thing that could happen? Your pants fall down? You trip and fall on your face? Your balls accidentally bounce off a spectator's head? No. The thing that terrifies jugglers most of all is the drop. That's right, unintentionally dropping a prop at the wrong time can be most humiliating.

Imagine yourself standing on stage in front of a hundred curious onlookers. They're expecting to see a skilled juggler, and you spill your beans all over the floor. What would you do? Scream and run off the stage? Swear? Hide the prop under your foot? Jump up and down violently on the prop until it disintegrates?

All of these are possibilities, but you should do none of them. The most common reaction by a novice is to turn red and stutter or make some feeble apology. Such a reaction will kill your presentation. You want your audience to laugh, not feel sorry for you.

You need to keep your act running smoothly. A good routine needs to be fast paced and flow without interruptions. Delays are annoying and distracting. An unexpected interruption is like dropping an ice cream cone as you're about to take a lick. Like the ice cream, your jokes are enjoyed and savored; a drop can be an unwelcome distraction.

How do you avoid drops? You don't. Drops are a part of the business. If you juggle, you drop, there's no way around it. Although constant practice will polish your skills to the point where drops are less likely, you don't need to be a flawless juggler before going public. What you will need, however, is a reservoir of *smoothies* or *savers* to help you out.

A smoothie is an apparent "ad-lib" performers use when a joke gets nothing but confused stares or when a trick backfires. When a joke flops or when a prop is dropped, the performer gets what is known as "flop sweat," a fever of humiliation which can destroy confidence and ruin the act. Using an ad-lib at such a moment will save your act and keep it running smoothly.

Does this mean you must be a quick wit and ad-lib in such a situation? No, few comedians are naturally gifted enough to improvise funny remarks all the time. Most entertainers keep ready made one-liners on hand in case problems arise.

Having several one-liners or savers ready for use not only rescues you from a potentially embarrassing situation but makes you look quick witted and clever. It also gives you self confidence, knowing that if a problem occurs you can handle it without embarrassment.

The inevitable drop will happen to you sooner or later. If you're prepared with a memorized ad-lib, you'll get a laugh. Your audience may even think the drop was part of your act. If the drop is handled smoothly, they won't even remember it after the show. Instead they'll remember how funny you were and that they had a good laugh. I've dropped props purposely just so that I could use some of my favorite dropped prop lines.

Memorize several dropped prop lines so they'll be on the tip of your tongue when the need arises. Keep a file of one-lines for future reference. Where do you get them? Make them up. Or write down jokes you read or hear that might make good drop lines. The following examples will get you started.

Jim Moore

Can you juggle upside down? Marko Dzamtovski can. He is shown here performing a head stand while bouce-juggling three balls off a drum. Who said jugglers don't have imagination?

DROPPED PROP LINES

Point your finger at the dropped prop and say, "Do that again and you're fired!"

•

"I may look bad, but I'm really much worse than this."

•

Yell, "Look at that!" Point to the back of the room. As the audience turns around to look, quickly pick up the prop and continue juggling.

•

Bend down to pick up the prop and say, "This act is beginning to pick up."

•

"Sometimes I does, sometimes I doesn't, and sometimes I does it a dozen times before I does it!"

•

Stomp on the dropped prop with your foot and say, "There, that'll teach you! Now get back up here!"

•

"I've only messed up on this trick once before—of course, this is only the second time I've tried it."

•

"I just washed these things and I can't do a thing with them."

•

"I learned to juggle in school . . . I missed the lesson on catching."

•

When the prop drops, scream, pick it up quickly, and shove it in your mouth. While holding it between the teeth, take several exaggerated deep breaths. Finally, take the prop out of your mouth and say, "Artificial respiration."

•

Pull out a large book with the words *HOW TO JUGGLE* printed on it. Read a few pages and say, "Oh, so that's how it's done." Put away the book and continue juggling. If you drop again, pick up the book and tear out the page, wad it up, and throw it away.

•

Squint your eyes and look around on the ground for the dropped prop. Make it appear as if your poor eyesight is preventing you from finding the prop. After looking without success, pull out a pair of giant eyeglasses and put them on to help you locate the prop.

•

"When I was shaving this morning, I must have cut my juggler vein."

•

After dropping a prop, quickly grab something else, like your shoe or hat, and continue juggling as if nothing happened.

•

Ignore the drop and continue juggling as if nothing happened. After a few seconds look at your hands, stop, and say, "Why didn't you tell me I dropped one?"

•

"That was my first drop today . . . hiccup."

•

If you're juggling clubs, pick up the dropped club, hit yourself over your head with it, and say, "Take this— Ouch! And don't do that again!"

•

Look apologetically at the audience and say, "Honestly, it's hard to find good help nowadays."

•

Look at the prop and say, "And where do you think you're going? . . . No, it's not time for lunch. Get back up here!"

•

Take out an oil can and lubricate your elbows. "It's been a while since I've tried this trick and I'm a little rusty."

•

"If I'd practiced more, I wouldn't have dropped it. But too much practice has side effects. An old Chinese wise man once said, 'He who keeps his nose to grindstone end up with flat face.'"

•

"I don't understand what went wrong. I just bought these balls. The salesman told me it was a good buy . . . Yeah, 'good-bye' ten bucks!"

•

"I did that on purpose. I was just testing the law of gravity."

COMICAL RETORTS

Often when juggling for friends or small groups, you will be asked questions such as "How long have you been juggling" or "where did you learn to do that?" You could give them a boring straight answer, but why do that? Remember you're a juggler, a unique individual, and

Francis Brunn, a former Ringling Bros. and Barnum & Bailey juggler, strikes a pose for the camera.

people expect you to be witty. Uphold your image as a screwball and give them an off-the-wall reply.

The best way to do this is to have a few preplanned ad-libs ready and waiting. Just as you do for dropped props.

The following are some examples of smart comebacks to use for probing questions from onlookers. Some remarks may sound abrasive if said in a bland way, but you will find that by putting a smile on your face and speaking in a jolly tone, you can say most anything and get away with it. Adding a contorted facial expression and physical movement will enhance any joke. Here are a few typical questions and answers.

Are the balls you use special?
No my hands are.

Where do you get your juggling balls?
From a Magician.

How come you can do it and I can't?
Because you haven't any talent.

Do your arms get tired?
Yes, but not from juggling

Can I learn how to do it?
I doubt it.

How do you do that?
Very quickly.

Can you juggle and eat an apple?
Yes, but not at the same time.

Can you juggle chain saws?
Only by proxy.

Have you ever had any accidents while juggling knives?
Yes, I once wiped out three spectators who asked too
 many questions.

Have you ever caught the wrong end of a machete?
Only once.

Can you juggle three bowling balls?
Yes, one at a time.

Are those machetes real?
No, their balloons in disguise.

Are you a juggler?
No, I'm an parrot in disguise.

Are those knives sharp?
No, I am.

How many objects can you juggle at one time?
Fifty-three thousand hairs is my max.

How many clubs can you juggle?
Two more than you.

Can you balance something on you ear?
Yes, my thumb.

Can you balance a club on your chin?
No, but I can balance my tongue between my teeth.

"Yee-haw!" cowboy juggler Hamilton Floyd spins his rope while balancing on a rola bola. It's almost as fun as riding a real horse.

Art Werger

What's the largest thing you can juggle?
Why, do you want a ride?

What does your wife think about your juggling?
She doesn't know I do it. She thinks it's just a nervous twitch.

Where did you learn to do that?
From the Wizard of Oohs and Ahhs.

Where did you learn to do that?
From my grandmother.

How long does it take to learn?
About 400 years.

Is it hard to learn?
No, anyone with half a brain can do it . . . would you like
to try?

Can you teach me to juggle?
No, I'm a juggler not a magician.

Use the answers and dropped prop lines I've give in
this chapter or make up your own. You may come up with
funnier lines. After all the juggling you've been doing by
now, your funny juices should be flowing wildly and you'll
probably come up with some real goobers.

5

ADVANCED GOOFONICS

You can juggle three balls, do a few tricks, tell some jokes, but you want more. Right? OK, I'll show you how to juggle things other than balls and bags, and I'll even explain how to juggle more than three objects.

One of the joys of juggling is learning new tricks and getting "oohs" and "ahhs" from friends. Also, knowing more tricks allows you to add new jokes to fit your newly developed skills.

This chapter is not for the squimish. For all of the tricks described here you'll need a good deal of practice to reach a moderately proficient level of performance. But if you've been goofy enough to read this far, you'll probably be goofy enough to try the stuff in this chapter, and may even accomplish some of the tricks described.

JUGGLING CLUBS

Contrary to popular opinion, a juggling club is not a prestigious organization restricted to jugglers. A juggling club is a prop that resembles a bowling pin, and most professional jugglers use them. Why do many jugglers prefer clubs? One reason is that clubs are larger than most juggling balls, making them easier for an audience to see. But the major reason is that the spinning motion of the clubs makes even the simple cascade a dazzling sight. Tricks performed with clubs are also more impressive.

Edward Jackman juggles four clubs while balancing a bicycle on his forehead.

The nice thing about clubs is that if you can juggle three balls, learning to handle clubs is a snap. It may take you a couple of hours' practice to feel moderately comfortable, but juggling clubs is easy compared to learning to juggle balls for the first time.

In order to juggle clubs properly, you must add a spinning motion, which keeps the clubs in balance as they are tossed from hand to hand. Juggling the clubs without this spin is extremely difficult.

Start by taking just one club into your right hand. Toss it in the cascade pattern, just as you did with the balls (Figure 5-1). As you toss the club to the other side of your

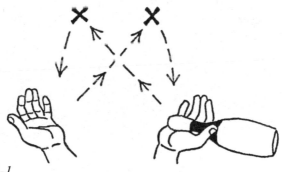

Figure 5-1

body, give it a little flip so that it starts to spin. Put just enough spin on the club so that it makes one, and only one, revolution by the time it is caught with the left hand (Figure 5-2). You could put two or three spins on the club if you wished, but that's for advanced club juggling. Stick with one spin for now.

Figure 5-2

You may find tossing the club for the first time to be exciting (it doesn't take much to amuse a juggler). Practice tossing one club in the cascade pattern until you become bored (about five minutes or so). If you're still amused after ten minutes—STOP! You're too goofy to go any further. Try golf or tennis instead.

Pick up two clubs, one in each hand, and try a simple exchange. It will feel awkward at first, but you'll get the hang of it after a few minutes of practice. Remain at this step as long as you feel it is needed, because the next step is a doozy.

For the final step you will juggle all three clubs. Put two in your right hand and one in your left, and let 'em fly. Toss them in the cascade pattern, just as you would toss three balls. The first couple of times you try this, you may scream and duck. This is an uncontrollable habit that many jugglers develop. Besides, a spinning club has a close resemblance to an airplane propeller and can deliver a mean whack to the side of your head.

If you weren't goofy before attempting clubs, you'll likely be that way after a few misthrown clubs collide with your brain. But with practice, your timing and accuracy will improve and you'll be juggling clubs like a center-stage showman.

MISCELLANEOUS OBJECTS

Do you want to really impress your friends? What about juggling something dangerous, like a machete.

Once you can juggle clubs, you'll be able to juggle most any other type of object, regardless of its shape. All elongated objects like sticks, machetes, axes, and even chain saws are juggled like clubs. A couple of minutes of pleasant practice, to get the feel of the object, is all that is necessary. But be careful! Clubs can hurt if they hit you, as you've already found out, but a machete can hurt deeper!

Another object popular with jugglers is the ring. Specially made juggling rings are available in sizes ranging from 12 to 16 inches. Like clubs, they must be thrown with a spinning motion. Rings are easier to juggle than clubs because the amount of spin does not have to be one exact revolution. The ring can be caught anywhere on its edge, eliminating the necessity of throwing a precise single or double revolution.

What about juggling other objects like fruit, shoes, and hats? You already know everything you need to know to juggle these objects. Anything that is roundish or small enough to fit in the palm of you hand can be juggled in the same fashion as ordinary balls. Larger nonspherical objects will need a spinning motion. Apples, oranges, and

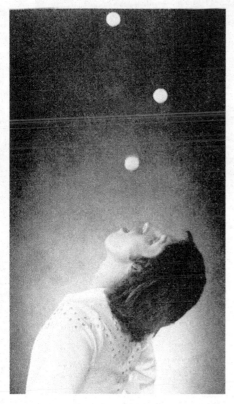

Anyone for tongue juggling?
Juggling ping-pong balls in his
month is just one of the tricks
Dick Franco is known for. He
can juggle as many as five
ping- pong balls with his mouth
as well as balance balls on his
ear, juggle four chain saws,
seven balls, and ten rings!

Three batone twirling – a
combination of twirling and
juggling. Corrie Jordan, winner
of the 1988 U.S. Twirling
Association's three baton title
shows her winning form.

Charlie Newton, I.U. Sports Photo

Bob Jones, performing his famous "thumb-stand" to demonstrate how using Boraxo soap tablets in his wash keeps his tie wrinkle free and in place throughout the day.

pineapples are tossed like balls. Hats and plates are juggled like rings. And, of course, large knives and other elongated objects are juggled like clubs.

Use your imagination and juggle some unusual objects like onions, celery, rocks, pajamas, and electric shavers. How about juggling bears, birds, piglets, and salad? You can do that, thanks to The Chasley Company. Chasley produces a series of unusual bean bags which make it possible to juggle bears, dogs, hamburgers, fish, and other objects. These bags are hand-sized and easy to juggle. So you can litter your house with flying cats, teach penguins to fly, and experience the thrill of a real tossed salad. If interested, write to The Chasley Company, P.O. Box 19202, Seattle, WA 98109, and tell them Dr. Dropo sent ya.

Juggling unordinary objects isn't a bunch of flapdoodle, it's fun and amusing. You'll look like a kook, but your friends will love it.

NUMBERS JUGGLING

Try tossing ten balls into the air and catch them as they come down and return them to the air as fast as you can. Seem impossible? It's not. As incredible as it sounds, a few seasoned jugglers have managed to juggle ten balls. Honest, I'm not kidding.

Such great feats of juggling mastery require not only natural talent but many years, and often decades, of dedicated practice. Only a handful of people have ever claimed to have succeed in juggling this many objects.

What about you? Are you one of the few individuals with the natural ability to develop into a ten-ball juggler?

If you are, I'll show you what you need to know to get started on the path to international fame. If fame and fortune are not your goal, maybe the excitement of being one of the few who can juggle four, five, or six balls is for you.

Four-Ball Juggling

The step from three to four balls is not difficult, however, it will require a fair amount of practice time.

Trying to juggle four balls in the cascade pattern does not work. You'll need to learn a new juggling pattern, which I will describe.

Take two balls in your right hand. Using just one hand, practice tossing and catching the balls by throwing them one at a time in a circular motion (Figure 5-3).

This is trickier than it looks. Give it a try and stick with it until you can toss the balls consistently in a smooth clockwise direction.

Now give your right hand a break and train your left hand to do the same thing in a counterclockwise direction (Figure 5-4).

Once you're able to juggle two balls in either hand, you're ready to try four-ball juggling. All you have to do is juggle two balls in each hand at the same time. Easier said than done, I admit, but if you're confident with each hand separately, combining them should not result in chaos.

With two balls in each hand, start by tossing one ball from the right, followed quickly by one ball form the left. In this way the balls are staggered so that you continuously toss and catch only one ball at a time (Figure 5-5).

Figure 5-3

Figure 5-4

Figure 5-5

Your first few attempts at this will look like havoc and you may feel terrible, but don't give up. It took me several weeks before I could do this movement comfortably.

Five Balls and More

Juggling four balls was fun? Now how about five, six, or more? You may ask, "Do I have to learn a new pattern for each?" Fortunately, no. You already know the patterns needed to juggle ten balls, or any other number you desire. Unfortunately, accomplishing the task is not easy.

To juggle any odd number of objects (three, five, seven, etc.), it's easiest to use the cascade pattern. For the five ball cascade, start with three balls in your dominant hand and two in the other. You'll need to move your arms faster and throw the balls in a slightly higher arc than for three balls. But that's how it's done.

To juggle an even number of balls (two, four, six, etc.), use the four-ball pattern I've just described. For example, to juggle six balls you'll need to practice juggling three balls in each hand and then combine them.

The first time you attempt numbers juggling it may seem impossible, but when you were a beginner so did the three-ball cascade. Give numbers juggling a try, you may find you have a natural talent for it. On the other hand, you may just look goofier. And that's even better.

ADVANCED TRICKS

By now you should be ready to learn some advanced juggling moves—tricks that will surprise and even shock your audience.

All of the tricks I will now describe have been attempted by jugglers. Many of them require no more juggling skill than being able to juggle three objects. Give them a try if you can, but I must warn you that some of these tricks are dangerous! If you attempt them, you do so at your own risk. Now that I've said that, have some fun and try 'em out.

Fire Juggling

The traditional method of fire juggling is to set three torches on fire and juggle them without screaming.

I prefer a slightly different method. I scream all I want. Also, instead of flaming torches, I use fire ants. I carry a pocket-sized ant farm with me so that I have them ready when needed. Fire ants are easy to carry and are not as hot as torches, which makes them ideal juggling props.

To do this trick, pick up three of the nasty little creatures and light 'em up. Setting the ants on fire makes the trick doubly dangerous. Besides, it keeps them from biting.

Wait for the flames to die down and then begin juggling. The crowd will go wild. You may too if you don't clamp the lid tightly on your ant farm.

Flaming Juggler

This is another fire juggling trick. Try setting your hair on fire as you juggle—it creates a spectacular effect. Even a simple three-ball cascade will look impressive.

One drawback with this trick is that I can only do it once every couple of months, and it gives me a terrible case of dandruff. But who cares? The show must go on, you need to impress that audience at any cost.

Moon Juggling

Fly to the moon and juggle. Because of the lower gravitational pull you can juggle 66.67 balls! Finding an audience may be difficult, but the real problem will be retrieving all the loose balls after a drop.

Although theoretically possible, this trick has not been claimed by many. The person who came closest to accomplishing it was astronaut Don Williams in 1985. In the space shuttle he worked on a project called "Toys in Space," in which he juggled six apples and oranges as he orbited the earth. This feat was carefully filmed and recorded by the most advanced scientific equipment and analyzed by the brightest scientific minds. Which goes to show that even scientists are goofy.

The Bugle

You don't juggle the bugle, you balance it on end with the mouthpiece on your lips. As it is balanced, juggle three balls and play "If I Were a Rich Man—I Wouldn't Be Doing Stupid Things Like This."

If you find it hard to play a tune on the bugle this way, do what I do—cheat. Replace the mouthpiece with a kazoo, forming what is known in musical circles as a "kazoogle." It will look like a bugle but sound like a kazoo.

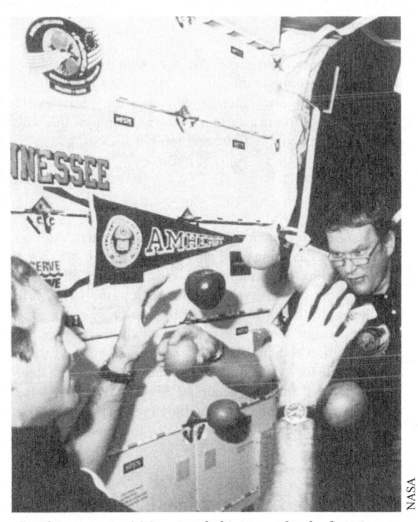

NASA

Juggling in space! Man juggled in space for the first time on April 15, 1985, but he ate the evidence! Don WIlliams, pilot of the NASA shuttle Discovery, manipulated apples and oranges in what he discribed as "a slow-motion act" as part of a Houston scientist's "Toys In Space" project.

Saxophone

If you're not into music, you may want to try this stunt. Balance a saxophone on your forehead and juggle three balls. Try juggling other objects as well. Vaudeville juggler Mac Morland used to balance a saxophone this way as he juggled a violin, bow, and top hat.

Banjo

Juggle three banjos. That's the easy part. As you juggle, pick the strings and play a tune.

You think I'm kidding? I didn't invent this stuff. Franco Piper did this type of thing back in the 1920s. He could juggle three, four, and even five banjos at a time while playing a melody. He would catch the banjo at the neck, position his hand on the correct strings, and give them a twist as he tossed the instrument back into the air. Other jugglers since then have copied his style. Some have teamed up to use six banjos in a duo juggling act. Where do you think the term "dueling banjos" came from?

Ice Cubes

Here's one trick that any three-ball juggler can do with a little persistence. Juggle three ice cubes until they melt. Voila! They're gone! You made them disappear like magic. Unfortunately, this trick is not very exciting to audiences.

Torpedoes

Juggle while balancing a torpedo on your face. Or just juggle three cannon balls without the torpedo.

So-called "strong-arm" jugglers have been juggling stuff like this for years. Both men and women jugglers have been known to balance and juggle heavy four-foot-long torpedo shells, cannon balls, and other heavy objects, even full-sized cannons.

Anyone can do it. It's fun, so long as you don't drop them on your toe. How do you think Donald Duck got his flat feet? He started out in show business as a quack juggler.

*Stong-arm juggler
Frank Elders with a
few of his toys.*

Dodo Bird

Stand on one leg, stick out your tongue, and juggle with your eyes crossed.

To do this trick right, each eye must watch the ball and the imaginary spot on the opposite side of the body. Lift your leg as high as you can, preferably up to your neck. Your tongue must reach out as far as possible in the opposite direction to help balance your body.

You may not juggle for long this way, but you'll sure look like a dodo.

Bird Juggling

Juggle live birds. You'll need to be quick to pull this one off. When tossed into the air, birds have a tendency to drift away.

It's also advisable not to look up when you're working with birds. They have no respect for jugglers.

Oatmeal Juggling

Grab a handful of cooked oatmeal, roll it up in a ball, toss it into the air, and begin juggling. As you toss and catch the oatball, it will break apart into two, three, four, and more pieces. The longer you can keep juggling, the more oatballs will develop. Keep going until you're juggling each individual oat.

The current world record stands at eight tosses. Can you beat it? Rush to your kitchen and give it a try, mom will love it.

Team Juggling

You'll need a friend to help you out on this one. Each of you take three balls. Have your friend place the top of his or her head on top of yours and balance up sidedown, and start juggling.

Boomerangs

Continuously toss and catch three boomerangs. You'll need lots of room for this one and quick reflexes.

Underwater Juggling

Swim to the bottom of a lake and juggle. This is much like moon juggling, except that you'll need to hold your breath longer.

Instead of swimming to the bottom of a lake, you can bring the lake to you. Fill three large balloons with water and juggle them over your head.

You can even get a partner and attempt team juggling with water balloons.

Assorted Objects

Try juggling as many different objects as you can. The most assorted objects juggled at any one time consisted of one chain saw, two swords, three hatchets, and four fingers.

Speed Juggling

How fast can you juggle? Using balls, count how many tosses you can make in ten seconds. The national record is 448. How close did you get?

Didn't do so well? Take three piping hot potatoes out of the oven and try juggling them. Your speed will improve dramatically.

6

GOOFY JUGGLING GAGS

What better way to make yourself look like a goofball than by telling goofy jokes? The purpose of this chapter is to start you off with some examples of typical juggling humor. I've entitled this chapter "Goofy Juggling Gags" because after you tell these jokes to your audience, they'll want to gag you.

This chapter contains many traditional gags that clowns and comic jugglers have used for years, as well as a few new ones. These jokes and gags will show you what many professional jesters use and will hopefully boost your own imagination into conjuring up other crazy stunts to impress your friends, or embarrass yourself. At any rate don't just sit there, get out your props and start practicing these gems.

HOW TO TELL A JOKE

Before I dive into actual gags and jokes, I'd like to give you a few pointers on how to tell jokes. Just repeating a funny story or a spouting out a clever one-liner isn't enough. To be really funny, you need to tell the joke in an amusing way.

Have you ever heard the same joke told by two people? When you hear it from one person you split your pants laughing, but from the other, the joke is a flop. Both joke tellers may have said basically the same thing yet one gets gales of laughs and the other draws only a few smirks, nauseated groans, or worse—cold silence. What's the difference? The difference is not so much the story as how the story is told.

The following techniques are used by professional comedians to make their jokes successful.

Keep the Element of Surprise.   What makes a joke funny? The punch line? Well, yes and no. The punch line is funny only if it comes as a total surprise. If people know what the punch line is or can figure it out before the end of the story, the joke is a disappointing flop. A good punch line will deviate from the expected or logical conclusion and hit the audience by surprise. When you tell a joke, choose the words you use carefully so that you don't tip your listeners off to the punch. This is very important. If the punch line is not a surprise, it's not funny.

Punch the Punch Line.   The punch line is the most important part of the joke, so make sure your listeners can hear and understand it. Often inexperienced joke tellers deliver the punch line with a last dying breath, or give it so quickly that the listeners can't understand it. Speak up and say it clearly. Give the punch line an little extra punch. Nothing will kill a joke faster than listeners asking, "What did you say?"

Personalize Your Stories.   Tell the story as if it happened to you. By turning the joke into a personal experience, it becomes more believable and consequently funnier. The audience may know you're feeding them a bunch of hooey, but it's more interesting to listen to a story told in this way than to hear about something that happened to someone else.

Make Your Stories Current. Make your jokes sound as if they occurred recently. A good way to give jokes newness is by saying something like "last weekend" or "just the other day." The assumption that the story has never been told before gives it greater impact. Even old jokes can be updated with current events and modern terminology to appear new.

Show Enthusiasm. Your listeners will listen to you in the same way you talk to them. Tell a story in a sleepy monotone voice and it will be listened to halfheartedly.

Express Feelings. Use vocal inflections to express moods and feelings. Avoid using words to describe anything that can be described with your voice. Take the following joke for example:

A woman turns to her husband and says, "I think your folks are trying to give you a hint that you should visit them more often."

"My folks!" he says in amazement. "I thought they were your folks."

The words "he says in amazement" are completely unnecessary in telling the joke. Leave out that phrase and show amazement in your voice as you tell the story.

"Ax-cues me!" Bob Nickerson juggling axes while balancing a pool cue on his head. Note his Oxford juggling shoes.

Art Werger

Show Animation. Use physical expression freely. Wave your arms, stomp your foot, express your thoughts with movement. Smile, laugh, cry, wince in pain, shout, become an actor as you tell your jokes. If you tell jokes like a stiff board your listeners we be bored stiff. Loosen up and bring your jokes to life.

Wait Out Your Laughs. Pause after telling each joke to allow the listeners time to laugh. Continue only after the response has died down. Don't wait too long, as that can slow down your pace, but too short of a pause will reduce your listeners' enjoyment. Continuing too soon may also prevent some people from hearing your next line.

THE WORLD'S FUNNIEST JUGGLING JOKES

I don't know whether these jokes are really the world's funniest or not, but it sounds a heck of a lot better than saying "A Bunch of Funny Things to Say While Juggling."

Many of these jokes are time tested and have been used by jugglers all over the world. That in itself should indicate that they are some of the best.

Much of the humor in these jokes comes from the tone of voice and the feeling put into them. Read the following jokes as if your favorite comedian was saying them. Imagine his or her mannerisms and tone of voice. Remember—don't just repeat a joke, tell it like you mean it.

Pull out three large knives and bravely ask the audience, "Would you like to see me juggle these?"

"Yes!" they say enthusiastically.

"WHAT!" you cry in terror. "Are you crazy? I'm not going to do that! I might get hurt."

•

When the audience applauds, look up and say, "You don't really have to applaud. I'm not going to quit until I'm finished."

•

Tell the audience, "I'm an excellent juggler, and to show you my great skills I will juggle six—yes I said six—things at one time. What things am I going to juggle? I will juggle six 100 dollar bills! But to do this I need your help. Does anybody have six 100 dollar bills I can borrow?"

No one in the audience responds.

"How about six 50 dollar bills?"

Still no one responds.

"Six 25 dollar bills?"

Look disgusted. "Well, then does anybody have six pennies?"

"Yes," someone will say.

Respond with, "Keep them. I hate to do cheap tricks."

•

"I took this trick out of a book called *Funny Juggling*. Everyone who sees me do it agrees that it's a good thing I did. It never should have been in there in the first place."

•

"Believe it or not, I'm one of the best jugglers in the country. All the good jugglers live in the city."

•

"I used to juggle three knives, two axes, a roaring chain saw, and a dill pickle, all at one time. But I gave it up because I didn't know what to do with my other hand."

•

This gag uses three rubber knives. Build up the audience for some spectacular knife juggling, but don't tell them that the knives are rubber. Begin juggling, and catch the blade ends rather than the handles. As you catch each knife, yell "OUCH!"

Put the knives down and show the audience the backs of your hands. Bending your fingers toward you as if you cut had them off say, "Looks like I just cured my nail biting habit."

•

"At a recent jugglers' convention, they had a contest to select the world's best juggler. I got Horrible Mention."

•

Pull out two balls and juggle them with one hand. Say, "This is what two-ball juggling looks like."

Then pull out a third ball and begin to juggle using both hands. "This is what three balls look like."

Add a fourth ball. "This is what four balls look like."

Finally, pull out a fifth ball, point to all of them in your hand, and says, "This is what five balls look like." Then put them down without attempting to juggle them.

•

Tell the audience that you'll perform some seemingly difficult trick, such as tossing one ball behind your back and over your head and catching it with your teeth.

Begin to juggle. Toss one ball behind your back and allow it to hit your head. React with a loud "OUCH!"

Pick up the ball and try again. This time throw it higher, and look up at the ball as it comes down. Open your mouth and let the ball bounce off your forehead. Again yell "OUCH!"

Rubbing your injured head, try the trick a third time. "Here we go. This time I will get it. Ready . . . set . . .

oh my gosh!" Scream, "Look at that giant bug!" Point off to the side, and as everyone turns to look, quickly place the ball in your mouth. "Ta-da . . . I did it."

•

Take out three unlit torches and ask, "Does anybody have a lighter?" Continue to ask around until someone gives you one. Take the lighter, stuff it into your pocket, and say, "Thanks . . . does anybody have a watch?"

•

"I haven't always been a juggler. I once owned a flea circus, but people said it was lousy. Some of them still say the same thing about my juggling, but I manage to scratch out a living."

•

"I was going to do a rope trick for you, but I decided to skip it."

•

"You'll have to pardon me, folks, for being a little late. I had a very embarrassing experience. I took my girl friend into a restaurant. We ordered, and the waiter brought the soup. My girl looked down and saw a bug in her soup. She screamed for the waiter and said, 'Will you remove this insect immediately?' The next thing I knew . . . I was out on the sidewalk!"

•

"To become a world class juggler I need to spend most of my time practicing, which doesn't leave much time for other activities. I used to go bowling every day, but not any more. I had to give it up entirely . . . well, not entirely . . . I still swear occasionally."

•

"I only do this as a hobby. I have several hobbies. One is keeping bees. I've been quite successful with it, too.

"What? You mean there's one on my head too?" Paul Cohen catching balls on his back and head.

Roger Dollarhide

Art Werger

"Hey, get yourself a pogo stick and come join us!"

*Cotton McAloon (left) does
the old balance three clubs
clubs on the face trick.
(Below) Nicolo the Gypsy
Juggler (Nick Newlin) and
Joanne Flynn, the
Queen of Whimsey,
demonstrate "huggling."*

Bill Giduz

M. Hauptschein

Never got any honey, but the bees stung my mother-in-law three times!"

•

After receiving a good laugh, say "I haven't heard a laugh like that since I came out on the beach in my swimsuit."

•

"I call this one my triumph trick. It's 90 percent TRY and 10 percent UMPH!"

•

"Now would you like to see my [name a trick] trick? You would? Good, because that's the only other trick I know!"

•

"I'm going to be famous, not for juggling but for my inventions. That's right, I'm an inventor. I just invented the cactus sandwich. You can eat it and pick your teeth at the same time."

•

"I do this next trick in answer to many requests . . . from my mother!"

•

"My grandfather used to be a juggler. He featured a trick with three empty jugs. The trick didn't amount to much, but he emptied a lot of jugs that way!"

•

"I've always liked show business. Why, I remember when I was only two years old, my mother took me to a freak show . . . but they wouldn't have me!"

•

"The man who taught me this trick was well educated. He had B.A. and M.A. degrees . . .er, not to mention B.O."

•

"I used to do this trick with an apple . . . but everybody said it was rotten!"

•

"One thing about being a juggler. I don't have an enemy in the world, nothing but friends. But some of my friends sure hate me!"

•

"After my show yesterday, one of the members of the audience came up and paid me a wonderful compliment. He said, 'There's more to your act than meets the eye.' I wonder why he was holding his nose when he said that."

•

"I'm not going to bore you with a bunch of old tricks like other jugglers do. I've got a bunch of brand new tricks I'm going to bore you with."

•

When juggling axes or some other dangerous objects, say "Folks, this trick is so dangerous that only one other living juggler is doing it today . . . and he's dead!"

•

When juggling any sharp object, say "I don't know how to do this, but I'm willing to take a stab at it."

•

Tell this one while juggling balls. "Last week I went to see a doctor. I said, 'Doc, I'm not feeling good. I keep seeing spots before my eyes.' He said, 'Well, that's nothing to worry about. Lots of people see spots before their eyes.' I said, 'yeah, but with me it's worse. Every time I see spots, I try to juggle them.'"

•

"Some jugglers have such great dexterity they can pick up a cent with their toes. But dogs have them beat; they can do it with their noses."

•

"As a kid I wanted to be a farmer and raise fruits. My friends tell me I ought to be on a funny farm. I guess that's like a farm for clowns. What do they grow on funny farms?—Why nuts, of course."

•

"I'm often told that I'm unique. I have something no other comic has—bad jokes."

CLASSIC SIGHT GAGS

These gags rely almost totally on physical expression and movement. They can be used with verbal accompaniment, but the humor depens on what is seen. All sight gags and even jokes are enhanced when accompanied by a goofy face or a silly expression. Go the the mirror and try out a goofy-looking face.

Hanky Panky

Sew a small rubber ball or golf ball inside a handkerchief. Before you juggle, stick it in your back pocket.

After a seemingly tiring move, stop for a breather. As you do so, pull out the hanky, wipe your brow then throw the hanky on the floor. The ball inside will make the hanky bounce back up, to the astonishment of all. Nonchalantly grab it on the rebound, stick it back in your pocket, and continue on.

Boomerang Juggling Ball

Attach a juggling ball to a pivot on top of a hat with about two feet of light fishing line. A plastic baseball cap works well. Secure the hat on your head and start juggling. The fishing line will not interfere with a normal cascade pattern. Nonchalantly toss the fixed ball out to one side. It will fly in a wide circle around you and return from the other side. As it comes around, catch it and continue juggling.

T-Shirt Bounce

This offbeat trick will make you look cleverly wacko. To do it, you'll need to wear a T-shirt.

While juggling, toss one ball high into the air. Hold each of the other two balls, one in each hand. As the third ball descends, grab hold of the end of your T-shirt and pull it out, allowing the ball to bounce off it. As the ball rebounds, let go of the shirt and continue juggling.

Hat Catch

You can do this classic juggling trick when wearing a hat. It makes a nice ending to a routine.

As you juggle, toss one ball up high in the air. Remove you hat. In one continuous motion, catch the falling ball and quickly flip the hat on top of your head without dropping the ball. Take a bow.

You can go one step further by tossing all three balls in the air, one after the other. Catch them in your hat and put it on your head.

The Human Fly

When using three clubs, stick one in your mouth and bite down on the handle, holding it between the teeth. Lift the other two up to your ears and wiggle them like ears (Figure 6-1). Blink your eyes and hop around. Looks so silly that it's funny.

Figure 6-1

Chicken Licken Juggling

You've learned about juggling apples, clubs, rings, and axes. Now you can try juggling chickens. Yes, chickens. It's not so hard. Take three chickens by the neck and toss them in the air. Watch them soar.

I find that live chickens get a bit finicky about this. You can try using dead ones, like from a grocery store, but they're a bit slimy. I prefer to use rubber chickens. Magic shops sell them. Inserting a wooden dowel into their mouths will stiffen them up so that they can be juggled like clubs. Three-chicken juggling—a great novelty stunt.

The Blob

For this gag you need two rubber balls and one clay or Play-Doh ball, all of the same size and color.

While juggling, toss one rubber ball onto the floor. As it bounces back, grab it and continue juggling. Do it again with the second rubber ball. Do it a third time but use the clay ball. When the clay ball is thrown on the floor, it will hit with a dull thud and lie there like a lifeless blob. Give a surprised double-take. Everyone will be shocked silly.

Balls on Your Nose

You will use three ping-pong balls for this stunt. In secret and before going in front of your audience, coat one ball with rubber cement and let it dry (about five minutes).

Also put a little rubber cement on the end of your nose. Don't worry it will peel off (the cement that is, not your nose). The cement will dry clear and will become unnoticeable and nonsticky. You are now ready for your demonstration.

Juggle the three ping-pong balls and tell your listeners that you will toss one into the air, catch it in a balance on the end of your nose. Being a goofy juggler, they probably won't believe you; such tricks are reserved for polished performers. The audience will probably believe that you'll purposely flub up.

Juggle the balls and toss the prepared ball up over your head. Bend back and let it fall gently onto your nose. When the rubber cement on the ball comes in contact with the cement on the end of your nose, the ball will stick in an apparent balance. You can then ham it up by swaying your head and body this way and that, trying to maintain the "balance." The audience will go wild with amazement. They thought you were a goofball, but here you are performing an incredible balancing trick.

While the audience is still shocked by your clever talent, straighten your head up and look at them. The ping-pong ball will stay stuck to your nose as you do. A funny sight.

End by sticking your thumbs in your ears and wave.

Balloon Balancing

This trick is very similar to the last one, but instead of ping-pong balls you will use a balloon. There are two ways to accomplish balloon balancing: 1) 300 years of constant, dedicated practice, or 2) use a bottle of rubber cement. I'll explain the second method.

First inflate a round, colorful balloon. Put some rubber cement on the balloon, covering an area about the size of a quarter. Next put a coat of rubber cement on the end of your nose and let it dry. Prepare your nose and the balloon in secret before getting up in front of your audience.

Explain that you're going to do a most difficult trick—balancing a balloon on the end of your nose. Bend your head back and place the glued spot on the balloon to your nose, so they stick together. Remove your hands. With the

balloon resting on your nose, gently sway your head back and forth as if trying to keep the balloon in balance. Listen for the applause.

As an added attraction, try juggling three balls at the same time. Finish by bending your head forward and looking straight at your audience. The balloon will remain stick to your nose. They'll bust a gut laughing.

Warning! Do not use super glue. When I tried this stunt with that stuff, the balloon was stuck to my nose for a month. It deflated after a week, but still hung on, dangling at the end of my nose. People would ask me what the wiggly thing hanging off my nose was. I was so embarrassed. I told them I was trying out a new punk rocker look. Believe me having a deflated balloon dangling from the end of your nose isn't chic.

Four Balls

This is a good gag for a quick laugh. Tell your listeners you'll attempt a very difficult trick—four-ball juggling.

Turn to pick up an extra ball. Out of sight of the audience, put a fake hand (obtainable at magic shops) into your pocket and place the fourth ball in it.

Now turn around to face your audience. Juggle three balls with your own hands while the third hand holds the fourth ball.

Egg On Your Face

This messy trick brings lots of laughs. Show the audience an egg and say, "I will now toss this egg high up into the air. When it comes down, I will catch it in my mouth without cracking the shell."

Toss the egg into the air, but when it comes down, let it smash into your forehead. Make a sour face at the audience as the egg drips off.

Eight Balls

Say boastfully to the audience, "I can juggle eight balls at one time." To prove your claim, pull out three billiard eight-balls and juggle them.

Nine Balls

"I will juggle nine golf balls at one time," you announce to the surprised audience. The golf balls, however, are stuck together in groups of three so that you need to juggle only three separate objects.

Rubber Eggs

To pull off this trick you will need to purchase three rubber eggs from a magic store. Place the rubber eggs in an egg carton containing several real eggs. In front of the audience take out two rubber eggs and one real egg. Before juggling, "accidentally" drop the real egg on the floor. This shows the audience that you are using real eggs. Step around the mess and take another rubber egg from the carton. Begin to juggle them.

Then toss the eggs to a spectator standing nearby and yell, "Here, you try it!" The spectator will jump, thinking the eggs are real. His reaction and the realization that the eggs are fake will bring a good laugh.

Blind Date

Three balls are used to give the juggler a funny face. Prepare your balls beforehand by drawing a large eye on two of the balls and a pair of big lips on the other.

While juggling for your group of admirers, stick the ball with the lips into your mouth and hold the two "eyeballs" over your eyes. Then say to someone, "Hello cutie, are you my date?"

Three famous jugglers from the turn of the century. (clockwise) Micheal Jara hittinh his companion on the head, Rubert Ingalese holding youthful assistant, and Richard Eckert. As you can see from the stunts shown here even in the old days jugglers were goofy.

Nutty Juggler

This trick requires a little preparation. Take a block of wood and cut it into a hexagonal shape. Drill a large hole in the center and paint it silver. It will now resemble a huge mechanic's nut. Make three of these. As you juggle them, you can say something like "Some people say I'm a nutty juggler. I'm not really, I'm just a little screwy." Make a funny face and act as though you're screwing one of the nuts onto the top of your head.

Froggy

Bend your head back and bring one ball up toward your nose as you say, "I will now balance this ball on the tip of my—gag . . . choke!"

Open your mouth and pretend to pull out a small green rubber frog (obtainable at novelty shops). "Sorry about that—I had a frog in my throat."

Hold up the frog and say, "That's not so bad. I usually end up with my foot in my mouth."

Eating the Banana

One of the all-time favorite juggling tricks is eating an apple while juggling. As a lead into this trick, you might say something like this:

"I used to juggle and eat an apple at the same time, but I haven't done that trick since the time I found half a worm in my apple core. That didn't bother me so much. It's what happened to the other half of the worm that made me sick. So now I use a banana."

Pull out a peeled banana and begin to juggle it. While attempting to eat it, open your mouth and cram the banana into your eye. Make some funny faces and wipe the banana off. "Maybe I will try the apple."

Now do the apple-eating trick, to the delight of the audience.

Three Apples

Say, "I will now demonstrate for you the famous apple-eating trick. I will use not just one apple or two, or four . . . but three."

Throw three apples into the air. As you juggle them in the cascade pattern, bend your head forward and try to bite one, but miss. Try a second and a third time without success. Finally, juggle two apples in one hand while casually eating the third with the other hand.

The Swinging Ball

Attach a piece of fishing line to one of your juggling balls. Tie the other end of the line to your belt. While juggling, drop the prepared ball so that it swings down between your legs. As it swings back, catch it and continue juggling.

Attached Balls

This is a good gag with three or more balls. You don't even have to know how to juggle to work this trick effectively.

Before the show attach a piece of string to each ball. Make each piece of string about two feet long and tie a loop at the other end. Make the loop just big enough to slip over one of your fingers.

Build up the audience for some fancy juggling; be serious so they won't suspect anything. Take out the balls, candidly slip the loops on your fingers, and hide the string in your palms underneath the balls. Now toss the balls up and let them fly wildly up and down as you pretend to juggle. This is really a funny stunt and looks best with four or five balls.

7

THE STRANGEST JOB
I EVER TOOK
A Visit to an International Jugglers Association
Convention by Shamus Flatfoot
(as told to Bill Giduz)*

July 17, 1984. It was a quiet Monday morning in Las Vegas. My partner and I were dozing when the phone rang. I jumped with a start, leaving a beautiful dame and a gin and tonic on a Pacific island beach in my dream. My cup of coffee spilled all over my shirt. I cursed at the way the week had started.

The phone call took me by surprise. "You want me to do what?!" I couldn't believe the Showboat Hotel manager on the other end of the line. "Serve as nursemaid to a bunch of jugglers?! You gotta be out of your mind!" Then I remembered that the rent was due and the man from the electric company was showing up at 10 to cut off the power. "OK, OK," I grumbled.

Checking registration cards isn't exactly my specialty, but neither is starving on the sidewalk.

"Stall the electric company and run some more water through the coffee grounds," I told my partner, then grabbed my straw fedora and headed out the door.

---

* Shamus Flatfoot, aka Bill Giduz, is the publisher of *Juggler's World* magazine and a past president of the International Jugglers Association. This is an adaptation of an article that apeared in *Juggler's World* after the 1984 IJA convention in Las Vegas, Nevada

It had another hole in the brim. Even the moths in the office were getting pretty hungry.

Freemont Avenue, the main road to Los Angeles. The Showboat was the first big gambling stop for all those weekend suckers coming out of California. It's not Caesar's Palace or Circus Circus, but you can lose just as much money there as anywhere. It had started raining by the time I pulled into the parking lot. It was the first shower in about 100 days. "Maybe it'll drown those cockroaches," I thought hopefully.

I strolled across the casino floor to the sports pavilion, where I was supposed to set up shop. The management had strategically positioned buckets on the floor to catch the rainwater dripping through the roof. I casually dropped a quarter in a poker machine as I passed by. If I hit a royal flush, I could go home and forget this weird assignment. Drat! No luck.

Resigned to my fate, I rode the escalator up to the second floor.

The sports pavilion was big and dimly lit. The only time I had seen it before, it had been filled with chairs and cigar smoke. Hot lights had shone down on the center ring, where two boxers pounded each other's brains out. That was my kind of excitement! I didn't know what to think about this juggling stuff.

Nobody seemed to be around. I was standing in the doorway, just about to make a break back for home, when a walrus-looking fellow walked up and introduced himself as Rich Chamberlin, "convention chairman and IJA secretary!" he said cheerily. I later found out that he taught school and operated a magic shop. He seemed harmless, but I wasn't sure.

Rich stationed me at the door.   Curious about the nature of the assignment, I asked, "If someone tries to get in without a badge, should I rub 'em out or just rough 'em up a little?"

"No, just send them on back to the registration desk," Rich replied.

"What a bunch of lightweights!" I muttered to myself.

Before the week was over, 503 people registered and another few hundred curiosity seekers walked in for a peek. I'm proud to say no one got in who shouldn't have. Rich told me the hall was going to stay open all day and all night until next Sunday. I felt like complaining, but I had a reputation to uphold, so I kept my trap shut and sent out for a ten-gallon urn of coffee.

About the time it arrived, so did all these people. One of the first characters I saw (but only the first of many characters!) was Jim Neff, who came walking up with his head cocked sideways and a ball resting on his ear! Can you imagine that! When he shook my hand, he tipped his head and the ball rolled up to his forehead! Geeez!

Everyone had a bag slung over their shoulder. I was gonna start inspecting them for explosives and guns, but Rich told me that wasn't necessary. It turned out to be a pretty friendly crowd after all. They looked like any group of Las Vegas tourists—until they started unloading their bags and playing around on the floor.

When I looked around and saw this 11-year old kid, Anthony Gatto, juggling seven balls while standing on a guy's shoulders, I knew I'd better start paying attention! So I got to know a few of them, and let me tell you, these jugglers are alright people!

Take Andrew Conway. He's an alien. What I mean is, he's from England, but now he runs computers in San

Eleven Year old Anthony Gatto juggling eight rings at the Las Vegas convention.

Art Werger

Mark Nizer balancing a ball on his ear.

Art Werger

Art Werger

Renegade Rene shows her unique style of catching clubs between her ears.

"I thought college fraternity initiantions were tough, but this IJA is ridiculous!" Larry Vaksman demonstrating his juggling technique.

Roger Dollarhide

Francisco. Not one of the best jugglers there, but plenty jolly. Dick Crowshaw told me that thinking about juggling was the only thing that kept him sane as he installed titles in sweaty little motel bathrooms down in Florida. Florida! Geeze! That's a long way to come to get your jollies!

There were other Florida people, too. Keith Watson and Ed Kosco juggle in Tampa as the Jasper Juggling Company. Seems their specialty is squashing melons. Yecch! What a mess! They impressed me, though, when they passed machetes back and forth while standing on rola bolas!

This girl with 'em, Jolene Koby, was a cook in the Navy and didn't even juggle when she got there. But she did by the time she left! She jumped in and helped out with the videotaping, too. That was typical. These guys seemed pretty unorganized, but people were always ready to help. It reminded me of a family reunion—I mean the regular kind, not like the one with the Gambinos in Chicago.

The videotapes were better than anything I ever saw on "Monday Night Football." This guy Barry Bakalor, ran them nonstop in a little side room, and a couple of the propmakers had some too. I couldn't sneak away to see many, though, because I had an important post to guard.

I almost turned back Andrew Allen, a weird-looking kid with orange hair dressed all in black. I thought he might be a subversive or something, but he turned out to be alright. Heck of a juggler, too! You couldn't keep up with his hands when he did his three balls. Dancing, shucking, and jiving all over the floor!

Talk about all over the floor, you shoulda seen Scott Burton. He was lying on his back juggling balls between his legs! These people were used to all sorts of things, but let me tell you, that turned a few heads beside mine!

Nowell Franco was this young girl who musta been a champion jump roper in another life. I saw her toss this diablo thing up in the air and jump over the string twice before she caught it again!

A fellow named Todd Strong from Seattle told me he used to sell 2,000 of these things called "devil sticks" a year, but was out of the business now. He's hoping they'll become folk toys. After trying to learn how to use it, though, I doubt it. I also know why they call it a devil stick—it's the devil to handle!

Not even flowerpots were out of place. Dale Jones was tossing up and catching five of them. He claimed I'd never see it anywhere else and, so far, he's right!

Just about everybody there could handle three or four of something, and a lot could handle five. But there were a few people trying outrageous things! Maybe I was hallucinating from no sleep, but by midweek I think I saw Dan Bennett toss 10 bean bags in the air and catch them. Robert York was practicing the same thing, and Albert Lucas showed it off in a workshop on Saturday. He did ten rings as well, and said he would've done 12 but didn't have enough ceiling height.

Lucas was sort of a hero. He won six of the eight championships he entered, and ended up spending a lot of time on the convention floor between his shows at the Hacienda Hotel. I think he was glad to be off his ice skates and standing on concrete, to tell you the truth. He sure took to the cinders like a fly to honey. I heard he won this 100-meter race where you juggle and run at the same time! They call it joggling. The sucker did it in under 13 seconds for some kind of record. He also kept

Bill Giduz

The traditional Big Toss-Up at the 1988 IJA convention in Denver, Colorado

juggling five clubs for more than 21 minutes. I mean, that's impressive and all, but it's about as exciting as watching cars pass on I-15!

A bunch of other people were pointed out to me as stars in the juggling galaxy. Lucas's brother David Lee was there and won the Juniors Championship. He started juggling at age 3, and is only 15 now. He said he could throw up and catch 10 rings. He and another Las Vegas show juggler, Dick Franco, each bought seven clubs (I used to think they were bowling pins, but now I'm smarter than all my friends!) so they could practice for next year's championships.

A big strapping Argentine guy, Jose Armando Pueyrredon, came by after his show one night at the Holiday Casino and seemed awestruck by all the activity. I guess they don't have jugglers' conventions in Argentina.

One non-juggler who dropped by was Bambi, the "exotic artist" in the Armando's show at the Holiday Casino. My jaw dropped down to my shoe tops when she walked in the convention hall Thursday afternoon!

The IJA president, Bill Barr, shook her hand and led her away to introduce her around. I guess he deserved to be her escort; he was the only guy there who wore a suit all week.

Speaking of that, I heard a funny one from one of the non-jugglers who came up to see what the dickens was going on. He said, "Maybe these jugglers should do a little less cascading and a little more showering!"

I hadn't realized when I took this assignment what a prime viewing spot I would occupy, but I could see it all. This little fellow named David Deeble, a real hot juggler in his own right, pointed out some other big names to me as they passed by. Lotte Brunn, an outstanding and gracious woman, came in with her son Michael Chirrick. Gil Dova, a comedy juggler who's played all over the world, was there, as well as Rudy Cardenas.

A bunch of IJA people seemed to be pretty well respected by their peers, too. Allan Jacobs and Michael Kass, former champions, were there along with this outrageous comedian named Ed Jackman. A guy with a butterfly tatooed on his head, known as "The Butterfly Man," walked in complaining about how the airline had lost his baggage. I told him he needed a good P.I. to investigate, but he wasn't interested.

A very French guy named Arsene turned out to be very funny. Paul Bachman from Chicago said this was his first convention since 1979, and he categorized it as "mind-boggling." He was speaking of people like Bryan Wendling, Dan Holzman, Randy Pryor, and Susan Kirby.

In the public show, Kit Summers did the only hoop rolling I saw, while an old pro named Hamilton Floyd twirled a rope attached to a cowboy hat and juggled three balls while on a rola bola!

Another old-timer I jawjacked with was George Barvin, who attended the very first IJA convention back in 1947 in Jamestown, N.Y. He remembered that back then anyone who could juggle five clubs was sort of a Superman. We looked out on the convention floor and recognized at least a dozen people who could do it today.

George told me that for many years until the young people started to join the IJA in the 1970s, conventions were mostly social events, and a lot of folks didn't even juggle. They were a lot smaller, too with only 40 or 50 people. Looking out on the several hundred jugglers in front of us, he said, "I never dreamed it would turn out this way."

A reporter for The *Five Club Flush*, Ro Lutz-Nagey, came up at one point and asked me what I thought about the convention. My cool was beginning to crack, and I replied that I was pretty amazed. Apparently that comment wasn't juicy or articulate enough, because it didn't make the next morning's edition. I never could get used to hearing people say, "I read it in the *Flush*."

Bambi may have been the only person who entered that hall all week who didn't learn how to juggle. The whole hotel staff, including the maintenance man and the convention programmer, caught the bug.

This fellow named Professor Confidence came up to me on the last night and asked if I was ready to learn. "I have two left feet," I stammered weakly. That was the wrong excuse though; he said I only needed my hands.

I was in a pickle then. I was being paid to sit there, so I couldn't go anywhere. I made the Professor promise not to tell my partner or the the Las Vegas P.I. Society, then gave it a try.

And you know what?! It only took 10 minutes. I can do it, too! Here I am, a 55-year old chain-smoking non-juggler, figuring I left my athletic ability behind when I was included in the first cut from the Overton High School baseball team. The most athletic thing I had done in 40 years was tossing rocks at that stupid mutt who raids my garbage can, but I can juggle! Now there's one for Guinness!

It seemed like I was only just getting into things when the convention ended. I hadn't slept in 96 hours, but neither had they. People were being real friendly.

The Renegade girl, Rene, gave me a big smile and a peck on the cheek before her people packed up their shop and left. Geeze, did she look good in that grey tuxedo and top hat! All eight of them did, as a matter of fact.

So good, in fact, that this big muckety-muck for the Magnum Photo Agency in Paris, Rene Burri, took their picture on top of the hotel for the European Geo magazine. I'll have to get a copy of that, and the October Smithsonian, because another lady was there taking pictures for that magazine.

Sunday morning the hall cleared out, and Rich told me I could go home. One of the prop makers gave me a set of bean bags as I got ready to leave. I didn't realize how apparent it was that I didn't have money to pay for them. I thought I was sad saying goodbye to everyone, but couldn't really tell if I was just exhausted or whether I had had a genuinely good time. It didn't take long to find out.

The rain was pouring down in the parking lot, and Freemont Avenue was beginning to look like the Colorado River. It was immediately depressing. "Back to the grind," I growled. I was standing around waiting for someone to turn their back so I could steal their umbrella, when another feeling swept over me. It was warm and friendly, the memory of the wildest week of my life. "Hot dang! Hallelujah! Yippee!" I yelled, and took off into the rain toward the car, joggling my three bean bags.

CONCLUSION

Every year the International Jugglers Association sponsors a convention like the one described here. Attendance at a juggling convention is a unique experience where hundreds of jugglers meet to demonstrate their skills, make new friends, and teach juggling to interested beginners. The event lasts nearly a week and is filled with nonstop excitement, which includes workshops, shows, food, contests, and plenty of fun. Sleep is usually delayed until the following week, as activities often extend into the wee hours of the night.

If you would like to share in the excitement of attending an IJA convention, you can join the International Jugglers Association. Founded in 1947, the IJA is a nonprofit organization dedicated to the worldwide enhancement of jugging. The IJA, along with its numerous affiliated juggling clubs, sponsors regular meetings, workshops, and festivals worldwide. These organizations provide members with education, inspiration, and opportunities to display their skills. All members receive a discount on admission to the annual IJA convention and a subscription to *Juggler's World* magazine. If you're interested in knowing more about the IJA, write to IJA, Box 3707, Akron, OH 44314.

Would you like to learn more about comedy juggling? If so, I recommend reading my book *Dr. Dropo's Juggling Buffoonery*. In it I reveal more tricks of the trade and describe in detail several complete comic juggling routines, all ready for you to use. All of the routines are easy and all are funny. Some of the routines don't even require any real juggling skills, relying instead on comedy movement and dialog; easy enough for beginners but funny enough for pros. If you want to impress your friends or just make it rich as a professional juggler, this book will be your guide. You can get a copy at your local bookstore or magic shop. If you can't find it locally you can get it from Piccadilly Books, Ltd., P.O. Box 25203, Colorado Springs, CO 80936-5203, or online at www.piccadillybooks.com.

CPSIA information can be obtained
at www.ICGtesting.com
Printed in the USA
LVOW13s1142280217
525668LV00004B/286/P